C000186933

It happer

LINCOLNSHIRE

DAVID CLARK

Merlin Unwin Books

First published in Great Britain by Merlin Unwin Books, 2016

Text © David Clark, 2016

All rights reserved, including the right to reproduce this book or portions thereof in any form or by any means, electronic or mechanical, including photocopying, recording, or by any information storage and retrieval system, without permission in writing from the publisher. All enquiries should be addressed to Merlin Unwin Books (see address below).

Published by:
Merlin Unwin Books Ltd
Palmers House
7 Corve Street
Ludlow
Shropshire SY8 1DB U.K.
www.merlinunwin.co.uk

The author asserts his moral right to be identified with this work.
Designed and set in Bembo by Merlin Unwin.
Printed in the UK by Short Run Press.

ISBN 978-1-910723-29-6

CONTENTS

Useful Addresses   iv

Map of Lincolnshire   v

Preface   vi

1. Introduction to Lincolnshire   1

2. Myths & Legends   12

3. The Lincolnshire Landscape   23

4. Into Battle   35

5. Crime & Punishment   47

6. Curious Customs   56

7. Entertainers   65

8. County at War 1914–18   79

9. Ecclesiastical Lincolnshire   92

10. Pioneers   108

11. Bomber County 1939–45   122

12. Scientific Lincolnshire   139

13. Literary Lincolnshire   148

14. Rogues   158

15. Political Lincolnshire   168

16. Warriors   179

17. Engineering Lincolnshire   191

18. Mysterious Lincolnshire   200

Bibliography   212

Index   214

iv   **USEFUL ADDRESSES**

Visitor Information Centre
9 Castle Hill, Lincoln LN1 3AA
Tel: 01522 545458
www.visitlincoln.com

The Collection
Danes Terrace, Lincoln LN2 1LP
Tel: 01522 782040
www.thecollectionmuseum.com

Museum of Lincolnshire Life
Burton Road, Lincoln LN1 3LY
Tel: 01522 782040
www.lincolnshire.gov.uk/museums

Lincoln Castle
Castle Square, Lincoln LN1 3AA
Tel: 01522 782040
www.lincolncastle.com

Grantham Museum
St. Peters Hill, Grantham NG31 6PY
Tel: 01476 568783
www.granthammuseum.org.uk

Louth Museum
4 Broadbank, Louth LN11 6EQ
Tel: 01507 601211

North Lincolnshire Museum
Oswald Road, Scunthorpe GN15 7BD
Tel: 0174 297055

Grimsby Fishing Heritage Centre
Alexandra Dock, Grimsby DN31 1UZ
Tel: 01472 323345
www.nelincs.gov.uk/resident/museums

Ayscoughfee Hall Museum
Churchgate, Spalding PE11 2RA
Tel: 01775 76455
www.ayscoughfee.org

Baldocks Mill Heritage Centre
21 South Street, Bourne PE10 9LY
Tel: 01778 422775
www.bournecivicsociety.org.uk

Epworth Rectory
1 Rectory Street, Epworth DN9 1HX
Tel: 01427 872268
www.epwortholdrectory.org.uk

Woolsthorpe Manor
Water Lane, Woolsthorpe-by-Colsterworth, Grantham NG33 5PD
Tel: 01476 860338
www.nationaltrust.org.uk/woolsthorpe-manor

Burghley House
Stamford PE9 3JY
Tel: 01780 752451
www.burghley.co.uk

Battle of Britain Memorial Flight
Dogdyke Road, Coningsby LN4 4SY
Tel: 01522 782040
www.raf.mod.uk/bbfm/visitorscentre

Cranwell Aviation Heritage Centre
Heath Farm, North Rauceby NG34 8QR
Tel: 01529 488490
www.cranwellaviation.co.uk

Metheringham Airfield Visitor Centre
Westmoor Farm, Martin Moor LN4 3BQ
Tel: 01526 378270
www.metheringhamairfield.co.uk

Thorpe Camp Visitor Centre
Tattershall Thorpe LN4 4PL
Tel: 01526 342249
www.thorpecamp.wix.com/visitorscentre

Lincolnshire Aviation Heritage Centre
East Kirkby, Lincs PE23 4DE
Tel: 01790 763207
www.lincsaviation.co.uk

MAP OF LINCOLNSHIRE

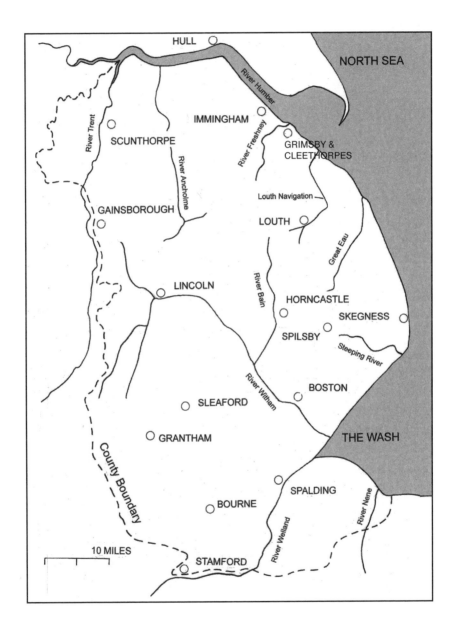

The rolling countryside of the Lincolnshire Wolds

PREFACE

On 17th June 2010, the *Lincolnshire Echo* reviewed a new book entitled *The Time Team Guide to the History of Britain*, covering 'everything you need to know about Britain's past'. Apparently, the authors had managed to compile it without making a single mention of Lincolnshire! Given the prominent role played by the county in the development of politics, exploration, science, literature and every other category of human activity one cares to mention, this, in itself, represents something of an achievement.

To be fair, television's Time Team have made many forays into Lincolnshire, but there are many other non-fiction texts, covering a wide variety of subjects, in which the word 'Lincolnshire' is astonishingly absent. *It Happened in Lincolnshire* seeks to redress the balance.

You may be unfortunate enough never to have visited Lincolnshire, and know little about it. Alternatively, you may live in the county and think that you know it well. In either case, read on. Inevitably, you will come to the conclusion that this book should have been entitled *It **All** Happened in Lincolnshire*.

David Clark

Chapter One

INTRODUCTION TO LINCOLNSHIRE

'Proud to be a Yellowbelly'

The county of Lincolnshire is the second largest in England (the largest being Yorkshire), measuring 75 miles from north to south, and 45 miles from east to west. The total area was reduced in the years 1974-96 when the highly unpopular county of Humberside was in existence but, with the north of the county back in the fold, the land mass has returned to its original size.

Lincolnshire's administrative divisions were once closely based on topographical features and comprised just three areas: Holland, Kesteven and Lindsey. Today, the situation is more complex, with a unifying Lincolnshire County Council, within which are several District Councils. In addition, there are two authorities – North Lincolnshire and North East Lincolnshire – created when Humberside was abolished. In 1901, the population of the county stood at 500,000. By 2011, it had increased to only 700,000. However, while population growth used to be focused on the towns, a good many of the larger villages are now themselves the focus of sustained development.

With regard to topographical features, it has been said that there are four words the stranger to Lincolnshire needs to know: Wold, Cliff, Fen and Marsh. The Lincolnshire Wolds, comprising a mix of low hills and steep hollows, reach out to the north-west of the county from Spilsby and Horncastle to Caistor and Barton-Up-on-Humber. To the west, they are bounded by the Ancholme fen, and to the east by the marshes on the coast. A second line of hills, called the Cliff, running from the River Humber to Grantham, provides Lincolnshire with one of its most prominent features. Although only 200 feet (61metres) in height, these hills form a sharp escarpment rising from the west, and afford panoramic views. On a clear day (so they say) it is possible to see York Minster.

The Fens reach out to the south-east from Lincoln towards The Wash. A second, isolated area, known as the Isle of Axholme, lies in the far north-east of the county. Both areas were originally swamps, created by the fresh water of river floods. The implementation of drainage schemes, initially unwelcome by the fen dwellers, turned them into rich and fertile farming land. It is this flat, arguably dreary, landscape which outsiders have come to associate with Lincolnshire. Why this should be is a mystery for, despite possessing its own charms, it constitutes only a limited portion of the county.

The Lincolnshire Marsh is the reclaimed land along the coast forming, as many writers have remarked, some of the most valuable grazing ground in the country. While material deposited by rivers, especially in the far south, has added to the land mass, erosion along much of the Lincolnshire coastline has taken its toll. Old Skegness, for example, disappeared beneath the sea long ago, while Mablethorpe and Saltfleet both had their churches washed away by the sea. It is thought that unchecked global warming could accelerate the incursions of the ocean to the extent that Lincoln might eventually become seafront property.

Lincolnshire was once thickly forested. By the close of the fifteenth century, the total amount of woodland was 35,000 acres. By 1900, this had increased to 45,000 acres. During the eighteenth and nineteenth centuries, tree-planting projects were undertaken by philanthropic individuals such as the Earl of Yarborough, who planted extensively on his estate at Brocklesby. Currently (2016), the total county tree acreage stands at 58,512, but an element of future uncertainty has been introduced with government schemes to sell off large tracts of woodland.

The drainage of the fens and marshes was bound to have an impact upon the survival of interesting and rare plants, but samphire is still prevalent on the coast. Sometimes erroneously referred to as a form of seaweed, it is often viewed as an essential component of the best menus. And wild cranberries, once harvested in abundance, are still to be found – notably at Friskney. With regard to fauna, the position today, thanks to proactive conservation, is rather healthier than it was a century ago. Writing in 1916, The Reverend J. Charles Cox notes that the buzzard 'has not been seen since 1855', and that 'the last bittern' was shot in 1848, while the short-eared owl 'disappeared about 1890'. Regular sightings today indicate that all have made a recovery. Seals, always a common sight along the Lincolnshire coast, are now actively encouraged at Donna Nook Nature Reserve. Similarly, butterflies have been provided with a habitat in a dedicated reserve at North Witham. Interestingly, Cox

'The Greyhound', Folkingham, one of Lincolnshire's celebrated coaching inns. Now converted into luxury flats, its glory days were in the eighteenth century, when it thrived as a staging post for coaches on the London-Lincoln run

also observes that because Lincolnshire is 'a great hunting county', there is not the slightest fear of the fox becoming extinct.

In respect of communications, Ermine Street, the main Roman road traversing the county, remains very much intact, despite suffering from twentieth-century runway extensions at RAF Waddington and RAF Scampton. Most of the major changes to the county's road network have been limited to the towns and cities, notably as a result of a perceived need to facilitate traffic-flow by the creation of inner-ring roads. Among proposals for future developments is an idea to extend the M11 motorway through Lincolnshire to the north-east of England. This would have a significant impact on the local economy and, in the long-term, could transform Lincolnshire into an urban county.

Today, Lincolnshire is served by its own airport – Humberside Airport, developed from the old wartime airfield of Kirmington.

Swan House, one of Boston's feather factories. Feathers were processed here between 1877, when the building was erected, and 1948

This is a far cry from the early nineteenth century, when the county was a complex patchwork of railway lines, many of the villages and smaller towns having their own stations or halts, where the stillness of a brief stop was broken only by the sound of a footstep crunching the gravel. The skeletal remains are a sad reminder of changing times.

The railway itself had superseded the canal system, which had once been of great commercial significance. The main canals – Stainforth & Keadby, Louth, Sleaford Navigation and Grantham – survive, but they are now used for recreational rather than industrial pursuits. Similarly, Lincolnshire's great natural waterway, the River Witham, served Lincoln's Brayford Wharf, the oldest inland harbour in the country, and a hive of industry, with warehouses, granaries, breweries and mills. The latter have now been replaced by the main University of Lincoln campus, together with a host of coffee houses and restaurants.

Tourism now constitutes an important part of Lincolnshire's economy, and the historical importance of heavy industry is often forgotten. During the First World War, for example, Lincoln made a significant contribution to the war effort, its factories producing prodigious quantities of tanks and aircraft. This was facilitated, in part, by the growth of the iron and steel industry in the far north of the county. The ironstone deposits of Swinethorpe and Frodingham had been exploited by the Romans, but were neglected and not rediscovered until 1859. Iron foundries were established and the first steel produced in 1912 in the new town of Scunthorpe. Just over a century later, the industry is in crisis and, like many another Lincolnshire settlement, Scunthorpe may have to reinvent itself.

Primarily, of course, Lincolnshire has always been a farming county. Potatoes, grain and vegetables of every variety, including continental imports like pak choi, abound. Mustard is not now so prolific and tulip and daffodil production in the south-east of the county has declined, as reflected in the demise of the annual Spalding Flower Parade, which gave its last display in 2013.

However, beetroot and celery are still valuable specialist crops, together with poppies. The latter were a source of opium, and they remain in demand for the manufacture of morphine.

Lincolnshire was particularly famous for its shire horses, the demand for which declined rapidly during the first half of the twentieth century. At one point, the breed itself was at risk, although there has been a slight increase in the use of the shire horse both for riding and as a working animal. Also at risk is the Lincolnshire Long-Wool sheep, once valued for its heavy fleece. The Lincolnshire Curly-Coated pig is now thought to be extinct, but Lincolnshire Red Shorthorn cattle continue to thrive, albeit under the shortened title of Lincolnshire Reds.

It follows that the county was also strong in agricultural-related industries. Cattle-cake was produced at mills in Lincoln and Gainsborough, and agricultural machinery was manufactured in Lincoln and Grantham. Factories processing feathers were particularly prolific; there were five in Boston alone.

One of the saddest declines is that of the fishing industry. In the early twentieth century, Grimsby, with a fleet of over 500 vessels, was one of the greatest fishing ports in the world. Today, only a handful of trawlers operate from the port. Boston, too, once participated in the deep-sea fishing industry, but catches here are now limited to shellfish – and even this remnant of a once great industry is now threatened with extinction. In addition to sea fishing, Lincolnshire was also once famed for its freshwater fish. The remains of medieval fish ponds, once attached to monasteries and manors, created for the purpose of farming fish, are to be found throughout the county, and are a haven for anglers.

In terms of architecture, the old Lincolnshire guide books tend to concentrate, in some cases almost exclusively, on descriptions of the churches of the county. Reverend Cox divides Lincolnshire churches into three categories: those of the old Lindsey district which are often 'small and mean'; Kesteven with its 'multitude of fine churches' and Holland, where it is 'almost

A view of Lincoln Cathedral from Brayford Wharf

impossible to overrate the size and beauty of the parish churches.'
As the twentieth century progressed, and the church ceased to be
the focus of village life, more and more were declared redundant.
Some of these are in the care of the Lincolnshire Old Churches
Trust and the Churches Conservation Trust, while others have
been sold off.

In addition to Lincoln Cathedral, the jewel in the crown,
noteworthy flourishing places of worship include: St. Denis's
Church, Sleaford with a canopied rood-screen regarded as the
best in the country; St. Wulfran's, Grantham, with its outstanding
steeple; St. Andrew's, Heckington, with many exquisite features;
St. Botolph's, Boston, famous as 'Boston Stump'; Holy Trinity,
Tattershall, with its profusion of fine windows.

Forgotten churches, of which county guides often make little
or no mention include: the restored Baptist Chapel at Monkst-
horpe. Built in 1701, when it was expedient for non-conformists to
worship in out-of-the-way places, it has a full immersion outdoor

tank for baptisms; Brauncewell's Church of All Saints is all that remains of a deserted medieval village; St. Faith's, Kelstern, set on a hill in a field; St. Leonard's Chapel, Kirkstead, which has been described as 'one of the loveliest examples of 13th century architecture in our land'; Old All Saints in Great Steeping, hidden away at the end of an old track and surely one of Lincolnshire's best-kept secrets; St. Margaret's at Winceby was demolished long ago, but the foundations and a few gravestones in what was once the churchyard can still be seen.

Rare items to be found in the county's churches include: an hour-glass stand, by which the length of sermons would be timed, at the wonderfully appointed Church of St. Peter & St. Paul in Belton; the oldest (1921) RAF commemorative stained glass window in the country at St. Mary's, Welton; the curious one-handed clock face of St. Michael's Church in Coningsby.

One of the county's most modern churches is St. Michael's in Waddington, built in 1954 to replace a twelfth century church destroyed in a bombing raid. Another place of worship is currently (2016) under construction – a purpose-built mosque for Lincoln, expressing the county's growing cultural diversity.

The county's noteworthy non-ecclesiastical remains include the castles of Lincoln, Somerton and Tattershall, the latter, home of Ralph Cromwell, a splendid piece of brickwork of the fourteenth century. Non-military structures include the Jews' Houses in Lincoln and The Angel Inn at Grantham, which numbered Richard III among its guests. The stone manor houses of Great Ponton and Irnham remind us of the county's famed building material – Lincolnshire Limestone, still quarried at Ancaster.

There are many imposing buildings which, although in use until comparatively recently, now lie abandoned. Most people would agree that new uses should be found for architectural gems, and conversion into housing is one way forward. St, John's Hospital (the 'County Pauper Lunatic Asylum') at Bracebridge Heath opened in 1852 and closed in 1990. A number of the old hospital

The Coningsby village sign draws attention to the settlement's role as wartime bomber base and to St. Michael's Church, with its famous one-handed clock

buildings now form the core of a housing development. From 1902, a similar establishment – designed by G. T. Hine, who specialised in mental hospitals – operated in South Rauceby. During the Second World War, it was taken over by the RAF for the treatment of aircrew, and included a dedicated burns unit. Although Queen Victoria Hospital at East Grinstead is most closely associated with the wartime work of the plastic surgeon, Archibald McIndoe, his pioneering surgery was also carried out at South Rauceby. After the war, the hospital reverted to its former use, eventually closing in 1998. It, too, is now a housing development, but many of the original buildings – including the burns unit – have been demolished, thus destroying a not insignificant part of the county's aviation heritage.

Finally, one must not forget the comparatively humble domestic dwellings which constitute Lincolnshire's villages – the real spirit of Lincolnshire, referred to by Arthur Mee as the county's gems – and gems they are, 'sequestered places which have delights and surprises for all who come upon them': Revesby, Faldingworth, Nocton, Kirby Underwood, Belton, Skendleby, Redbourne, to name but a handful.

This leaves only one question: what is the meaning of the phrase 'proud to be a yellowbelly'? A yellowbelly is someone who has been born and bred in Lincolnshire – and proud of the fact.

Tattershall Castle was developed from a traditional 13th Century castle by Ralph Cromwell, Treasurer of England 1433-43

Title holders can even acquire a 'Proud to be a Yellowbelly' sticker to affix to their car windscreens. Well-pleased they may be, but they will never agree on the origins of this most peculiar nickname. Many suggestions have been put forward. Some say that opium from poppies, prescribed as an early treatment for malaria (from which the Fen dwellers suffered) turned the skin yellow. Others argue that stage-coaches which served the county had yellow livery. The most likely explanation is a variation on the latter. Officers of the Royal North Lincolnshire Militia, formed in 1759, wore yellow waistcoats, and it is probable that their enemies called them 'yellowbellies', in the same way that Confederate troops in the American Civil War referred to the blue-coated opposition as 'blue-bellies'.

Chapter Two

MYTHS & LEGENDS

King John's Lost Treasure

In some ways – certainly as far as the popular imagination is concerned – we are more familiar with the period of King John's tenure as prince-in-waiting to the throne, than with the events of his actual reign. Permanently involved in evil schemes to supplant his elder brother King Richard III, who is absent fighting in the Holy Land, John is always outwitted by the resourcefulness of Robin Hood.

The single event of John's reign seemingly worthy of note is the creation of The Great Charter or *Magna Carta*, famously signed at Runnymede, near Windsor Castle, on 15th June 1215. Although much of the document is concerned with the rights of the barons, a number of the clauses were later proved useful in framing the principles of democratic government. A rare copy is housed in a specially-constructed vault in Lincoln Castle.

Overall, John's seventeen-year reign was not a success. Most of the crown's possessions in France were lost and king and barons were permanently in conflict. By the beginning of 1216, the king was in dire straits. King Alexander II of Scotland had come out in support of the barons, and Prince Louis (soon to become King

Louis VIII) of France followed his example. In his attempts to meet these challenges to his authority, John spent what proved to be the final nine months of his life constantly on the move.

The month of September 1216 found him in the rebel baronial stronghold of East Anglia. After relieving the city of Lincoln, which the barons had invested, he marched on to Kings Lynn. During military campaigns, it was customary for a king to take his treasure – including the crown jewels – along with him, as part of his baggage train. Sometimes, the baggage train, of necessity travelling slowly, trailed behind, but it is probable that John *was* with his baggage train when he returned westward from King's Lynn.

According to the contemporary chronicler, Roger of Wendover, as the king and his army were crossing the River Wellester – a long-since vanished estuary flowing into The Wash – 'the land opened in the middle of the water and caused whirlpools which sucked in everything'. John and his army were able to escape, but 'all his carts, waggons and baggage', including his treasure and the crown jewels were lost.

The night immediately following the disaster was spent at 'a convent called Swineshead'. Roger is referring to Swineshead Abbey, a Cistercian monastery founded in 1134. Here, John was 'seized with a violent fever', as the result of the anguish he felt about the loss of all his worldly goods. Nevertheless, he subsequently continued on his way, getting as far as Newark Castle, where he died on 18th October.

After his death, there were rumours that he had been poisoned. Raphael Holinshed, whose *Chronicles of England, Scotland and Ireland* appeared three centuries later, gives 'Wellestreme sands' as the location of the baggage train disaster and notes that a monk of Swineshead Abbey, 'being moved with zeal for the oppression of his country, gave the king poison in a cup of ale'.

Shakespeare used Holinshead as a basis for his own version of John's end. In the penultimate scene of *The Life and Death of King*

John – set in Swineshead – Hubert confides to Philip, natural son of the Earl of Faulconbridge:
> *The king, I fear is poisoned by a monk.*

And it is Philip, who has been fighting the barons on John's behalf, who suffers the loss of the baggage train:
> *I'll tell thee, Hubert, half my power this night,*
> *Passing these flats, are taken by the tide;*
> *These Lincoln Washes have devoured them;*

Historians believe that John died of dysentery and, given the symptoms of the affliction, it is easy to understand how the rumours of poison arose. Similarly, while it is likely that the baggage train incident did occur, there is no solid evidence that the royal treasure was lost. The real import of the story at the time lay in its utility for John's enemies who publicised the incident as just retribution for all the king's perceived wickedness – much as the punishment inflicted upon Pharaoh as the Egyptians followed the Israelites across the Red Sea:

> *And the waters returned, and covered the chariots, and the horsemen, and all the host...*

In the longer term, the baggage train has developed into a holy grail... It may have been lost near Wisbech or, alternatively, further west, in the vicinity of Sutton Bridge. If it does exist, it lies buried beneath centuries of accumulated silt, but this has not discouraged treasure hunters from trying to find it. Latest developments in LIDAR technology which combines laser technology with GPS data, showing the way the landscape has changed over time, may offer new hope.

Byard's Leap

Byard's Leap, off the Newark road, six miles to the west of Sleaford, is the scene of one of Lincolnshire's best-known legends. The story is as follows: A witch by the name of Old Meg lived in a cave with her two children. She was a malicious crone, making her neighbours' lives a misery by bringing down illness upon them and ruining crops. A local old soldier made it his business to do away with her. In need of an alert horse, he visited a pond where horses were drinking and threw a pebble into the water. The horse that reacted most quickly went by the name of 'Blind Bayard', and although it was, indeed, blind, the soldier chose it for his mount. Approaching the witch's cave, he called to her to come out. She replied that he would have to wait until she was ready. When she did appear, he struck at her with his sword and she sprang up behind him, sinking her sharp nails into the horse's flanks – spurring the terrified animal into making a prodigious leap of some 60 feet (18 metres). The soldier managed to bring 'Blind Bayard' under control, swung around and drove his sword into Old Meg's heart. There are many variations on this traditional tale. Sometimes, a shepherd plays the role of the old soldier. In other versions, 'Blind Bayard' is accidentally killed along with Old Meg.

The story retains interest because the spot where it all allegedly happened is marked by an information panel, adjacent to four horseshoes set in a small gravel plot, indicating where Bayard came to rest. A second set, marking the point where Bayard took off lie in a copse at the other side of the car parking area. A mounting stone, where the rider mounted the horse, can be seen across the road at the entrance to the farm complex. Legend has it that the witch's cave lies beneath the present-day garage.

The real interest in this traditional tale lies in the name of the horse. Bayard is a mythical beast which first appeared in the twelfth century, in the French *chansons de geste* ('Songs of Heroic Deeds'). Here, Bayard is a rather wonderful beast, having the ability to adjust its size to accommodate four riders. Although the steed of Byards Leap still possesses almost magical properties by virtue of the enormous jump it is capable of making, Bayard found its way into the English Language as a synonym for foolishness and reckless behaviour.

Thus, Bayard is the name of the foolish horse belonging to

One of two sets of horseshoes, flanked by an information panel, at the site of Byard's Leap

Troilus in Geoffrey Chaucer's fourteenth century adaptation of *Troilus and Criseyde*:

> But every day things that fools trust in end
> As proud Bayard begins to shy and skip
> From the right course…..

In *The Canon Yeoman's Tale*, Chaucer presents Bayard as a blind creature:

> You are as heedless as is Bayard the blind horse
> That blunders forth and takes account of no peril.

In 1532, Thomas More refers to Bayard in a similar sense in *The Confutations of Tynedale's Answer*:

> ….the Scripture, albeit many places be plain, and in the hardest place good folk may take fruit if they play not as Tynedale doth be bold upon it like Blind Bayard and think it plain and open….

Allusions were still being made a century later, in John Milton's tract *Doctrine and Discipline of Divorce*:

> …..being a bayard who never had the soul to know what conversing means.

A hundred years later, usage had declined. Dr. Johnson makes no mention of the word 'bayard', while *Bailey's Universal Etymological English Dictionary*, published in 1721, merely defines it as a bay horse. The *OED* revived the definition relating to blind recklessness or, as a proper noun, 'a self-confident ignoramus', giving the date 1529 as the first recorded usage in the latter respect.

'Bayard' is also used in several place names. In 1249, for instance, 'Baynard's Green' near Bicester in Oxfordshire was one of only three places authorised by King Richard I to hold tournaments. (In the mid-seventeenth century, the six-mile open stretch of land was still being used for horse-racing.) Similarly, it is probable that in Lincolnshire, the Knights Templar of Temple Bruer (see page 26) held tournaments in the locality of Byard's Leap. The legend may even have developed from some feat of horsemanship that occurred at one of these events.

Imps and Demons

Weekly local newspaper reports of the exploits of Lincoln City AFC often carry headlines referring to the 'Imps', for that is the club's nickname. It is derived from the Lincoln Imp which, as its name suggests, is currently the symbol of the City of Lincoln itself.

The Lincoln Imp has its origins in Lincoln Cathedral. According to folklore, a pair of imps – mischievous demons, regarded as the Devil's offspring – either by accident or design visited the cathedral. Entering the retro-choir, they embarked on an orgy of destruction, which was brought to a halt by the appearance of an Angel who turned one of the imps into stone. It remains transfixed in a seated posture, its hands holding its right leg which rests on the left one.

Its companion escaped and, according to some sources, made its way to Grimsby, where it entered the Church of St. James and commenced wreaking havoc. Again, an Angel came to the rescue and gave the creature a spanking before turning it to stone. Called by some, the Grimsby Imp, it can be seen (rubbing its sore rump)

The Lincoln Imp, in the Angel Choir, Lincoln Cathedral

above the marble altar in the South Aisle. In an
alternative version, the second imp made it only
as far as the south porch of the Bishop's door of
Lincoln Cathedral, where it jumped on a witch's
humped back. Both imp and witch were turned to
stone, as depicted in the carving above the door.
    The story of the Lincoln Imp also extends to
Lincoln College, Oxford. In 1899, the college was presented with
an image of the Lincoln Imp which stood in the front quad above
the doorway to Hall. In 2001, having become somewhat weather-
beaten, it was taken down and replaced by a new image. The college
magazine is called *The Lincoln Imp* and the boat club has taken the
Imp as its mascot. In addition, it is claimed that the Lincoln College
Imp gave rise to the phrase 'to look as the devil looks over Lincoln',
describing someone who speaks unfavourably of another.
    The popularity of the Lincoln Cathedral Imp dates from the
late nineteenth century with a Lincoln jeweller called James Ward
Usher. His father started the business, but it did not begin to flourish
until James assumed control. An astute businessman, he decided to
exploit the Lincoln Imp by using it as a motif for his wares. By
patenting the idea, he ensured that no one else could use it, and he
was soon producing everything from souvenir spoons to expensive
tie-pins and brooches. Although quite grotesque, they became very
fashionable. Even the Prince of Wales, the future Edward VII, wore
one of the tie-pins bearing a diamond-studded imp. Usher became
so well-known that it is said anyone who wanted to write to him
only had to address a letter to 'The Silversmith who makes and sells
the Lincoln Imp'. The items had the added appeal of supposedly
bringing good luck to the owner. They were certainly lucky for
Usher. The wealth he accumulated allowed him to make a bequest
which established the city's Usher Gallery, with its array of objets
d'art – much of it from Usher's own private collection.

Imps and demons can also be seen on the exterior of churches in the form of gargoyles – grotesque sculptures designed to channel rainwater away from the walls. Lincolnshire churches furnish many examples. For example, at St. Laurence's Church in Surfleet, a demon's head channels water into a drainpipe via its open mouth. St. Andrew's Church in Heckington has several such figures. The Churches of All Saints in Moulton and St. Michael's in Coningsby both feature fully-fledged winged demons – the latter figure functioning as a bracket to support a projection of guttering.

Gargoyles take many forms, and it would appear to be singularly inappropriate for demonic designs to be deliberately chosen to decorate places of worship. Stonemasons, who were generally given a free hand when it came to minor features of exterior décor, may just have allowed their imagination to run free. Alternatively, given that running water is traditionally recognised as an 'antidote' to various forms of supernatural evil, the image of a devil with water gushing from its mouth might have made some kind of sense to the medieval mind.

Still less satisfactory is the concept of representations of imps and demons being used to adorn the interiors of churches. Yet, they appear in profusion, the Imp, for example, being only one of many sculptures of devilish figures to be found within the retro-choir of Lincoln Cathedral. It is said that such images were provided to remind worshippers of the on-going battle between good and evil. Or perhaps the image of a demon waiting to pounce on the unwary was simply a useful tool for encouraging sinners to abandon their wicked ways.

The Usher Gallery, Lincoln

Set in Stone

Lincolnshire possesses very little in the way of ancient stones. Other counties abound these menhirs, standing singly as monoliths or severally as stone circles, and while Lincolnshire undoubtedly once possessed henges, there now remain what can only be described as a few oddities.

One strange stone of uncertain origin is the Winceby Stone, situated on the grass verge on B1195 near the hamlet of Winceby. It used to stand in the adjoining field, where it stood for centuries, having the reputation of being immovable. It was also believed that buried treasure lay underneath. From time to time, therefore, attempts were made to shift it. Collectors of folklore usually quote an instance in which several horses, yoked to chains fastened around the stone, almost succeeded in pulling it over. Then, at a crucial moment, one of the men standing by uttered an oath, at which the Devil suddenly appeared on top of the stone and firmly stamped it back into place. Scratches resembling claw marks on top of the stone were cited as evidence.

An alternative explanation for these scratches is that they were made by troops sharpening their swords prior to the Battle of Winceby (see page 43). The position of the stone coincides with the likely deployment of Royalist participants in the battle, and it is possible that the stone was used for such a purpose. In 1970,

The Winceby Stone, flanked by an information panel providing details of the English Civil War encounter, 'Winceby Fight'

with the aid of specialised lifting gear, the stone was moved to its present location. Instead of treasure, the removal team discovered a selection of broken ploughshares, suggesting that the stone was gradually uncovered during centuries of ploughing.

The Fonaby Sack Stone, like the Winceby Stone, once stood in the middle of a field, wreaking similar damage on ploughs. It now stands in the hedgerow bordering a farm track leading from Fonaby Top Farm, to the north of Caistor. The legend surrounding this stone concerns St. Paulinus, a Roman missionary and the first Bishop of York who died in AD644. One day, mounted on an ass, he was travelling through the area when he came to a spot where a farmer was gathering corn. Paulinus asked for some of the grain from a sack standing in the field. The farmer told him that it wasn't a sack, but a stone. As it was clearly not the man's intention to share any of his grain, Paulinus promptly turned the sack into a stone – and a stone it remained. Efforts to move it always brought ill-luck to anyone foolish enough to try. For example, one of the masons working on the construction of Pelham Pillar (see page 29) chipped a bit off to carve into a model and was promptly killed in a fall.

In its original state, the stone may have consisted of two or three separate blocks, the structure being broken up to facilitate transport, when it was finally moved in 1917.

The Drake Stones stand outside St. Edith's Church in the village of Anwick. Originally, they made up a single stone which stood in a field half a mile to the north west.

Legends surrounding it are slightly different to those focussing on the Winceby Stone and the Fonaby Stone. A farmer was supposedly ploughing a field when his plough and horses sank into the earth and disappeared from view. A drake flew out of the hole that was left in the ground. The next day, the farmer returned to find that a boulder, in the shape of a drake's head, had appeared in the middle of the hole. Tales of buried treasure, located beneath it in a cave inhabited by the Devil, and attracting bad luck to anyone foolish enough to search for it, also developed. During

The Drake Stones,
St. Edith's Church,
Anwick

the late nineteenth century, antiquarians suggested that the stone had druidical connections, constituting nothing less than 'a sacred object of adoration' for the druids. It had been chosen because of its egg-like shape – the egg symbolising the fountain of life. Furthermore, the name 'drake' had its origins in the celtic *draig*, meaning dragon, or the deity to which the stone was dedicated.

What seems to have happened is that the Drake Stone, like its counterparts, standing in the middle of a field, was a hazard to the plough. Instead of moving it, it was decided to excavate the earth surrounding it so that it could be sunk to a safe level. At some point in the 1920s, the stone was moved to its present location at the church. When it was uncovered, it was already in two parts, a smaller portion having broken off from the main mass. Some say that it did not acquire its name until after its relocation, when it was observed that two drakes were using it as a shelter.

In reality, it is probable that all of the above mentioned stones are glacial erratics, which is to say that that they were carried to their final resting places by glacial ice. In this context, it is interesting to note that the Drake Stone has a water-worn appearance and what appear to be traces of sea shells embedded in its surface.

Chapter Three

THE LINCOLNSHIRE LANDSCAPE

Draining The Fens

Attempts to drain the Lincolnshire fenlands date back to the Roman occupation. Interest in the subject was rekindled by the Normans. Those who had been given lands by the conqueror king, William I, were keen to render them profitable and, where necessary, dug ditches in an effort to dry them out. The monasteries also played a role in draining the lands which fell within their remit. The difficulty was that all of the early schemes were small, local ventures. Something on a far bigger scale was needed to turn these vast tracts of marshy waste into profitable farmland.

The model for the innovative drainage work of the seventeenth century was the scheme of Thomas Lovell for draining the Deeping Level in the reign of Queen Elizabeth I. Lovell financed the venture personally and, in return, was promised a portion of the drained acreage. He failed to complete the project because of resistance from local people for whom the fens represented a way of life. During the summer months, when the land was fairly dry, it was used as common pasture for sheep and cattle. There were fish and wildfowl in abundance and, of course, reeds for thatching. Folk even lived on the fens. Known as 'fen stodgers', they dwelt in constantly waterlogged huts and eked out a living by cutting turf and peat to sell as fuel.

King James I gave lip service to the cause of fen drainage, avowing that he would not permit the fen counties 'to be abandoned to the will of the waters', but it was his son, Charles I, who became the first monarch to persevere with the concept and to deal effectively with any opposition. Charles was Lord of the Manors of Hatfield and Epworth and, by draining the fendlands of Hatfield Chase and the Isle of Axholme in North Lincolnshire, he hoped to increase its profitability. To this end, he employed a Dutchman, Cornelius Vermuyden, who agreed to perform the task in return for a grant of one third of the land area.

The scheme was challenged by the commoners who would lose their rights of pasturage on all but a limited acreage. In support of their action, they produced a deed dating from the fourteenth century in which John de Mowbray, at that time Lord of the Manor, promised to undertake no further improvements schemes. (In itself, this is of interest, because it shows that drainage work had been in progress at this relatively early date.)

However, Vermuyden went ahead anyway. As a result, his imported Dutch workers were intimidated and physically assaulted by the locals. The king gave Vermuyden his full backing and punitive action was undertaken by the government to put a stop to

Fenland: The Isle of Axholme

the disruption. Nevertheless, dissatisfaction continued to express itself in sporadic outbreaks of violent disorder, which the shrewd Vermuyden alleviated to some extent by employing some of the malcontents at high wages.

Drainage of large tracts of fenland which had more than one (possibly recalcitrant) Lord of the Manor presented a more difficult problem. This was overcome by the imposition of a high tax for new drainage works. When the taxes were not paid, the land was seized and sold on to third parties who were more amenable to suggestions of the benefits of drainage schemes. In the south of the county, the Earl of Lindsey assumed responsibility for draining the Lindsey Level, receiving 24,000 acres out of a total of 72,000 acres for his pains. Drainage of the Wildmore, East & West Fens was contracted out to Sir Anthony Thomas. The king himself declared himself as the undertaker of Holland Fen, awarding himself almost a third of the 22,000 acres involved.

The drainage process itself comprised the digging of new channels to collect the water and on-going river-bed clearance coupled with maintenance of high banks to prevent watercourses overflowing. All this was achieved by hard manual labour although on occasions, windmill technology was adapted to help in scooping out river beds. Then, as now, wind power was not reliable, in addition to which all machinery was vulnerable to sabotage.

Certainly, there was money to be made out of drainage schemes, largely at the expense of people who depended for their livelihood upon common usage of the fenlands. On the other hand, drained acreages did produce generous returns in terms of basic arable crops, which worked to the benefit of all. The destruction of an ancient way of life was viewed as acceptable collateral damage.

Sadly, much of the drainage work undertaken during the early seventeenth century fell victim to the English Civil War. The drainage undertakings were in themselves the focus of much resentment against the king and, as such, constituted a contributory, albeit localised, cause of the conflict. Opponents of the schemes, using the war as an excuse to renew their attacks upon the works, wrecked many of them.

When the war came to an end, the fenmen not unnaturally expected government support, but their hopes were to be dashed, for Parliament merely made arrangements for new drainage schemes on the same basis as the late king. Nothing had changed.

The Knights Templar of Temple Bruer

The Order of the Knights Templar was founded in the year 1119. Its purpose was to protect pilgrims visiting Jerusalem (back in Christian hands since 1099, following the success of The First Crusade) from roving bands of thieves. Originally, the order consisted of only nine knights, who swore to 'guard the public roads, forsake worldly chivalry and, living in chastity, obedience and poverty...to fight with pure minds and hearts'. Wearing red crosses sewn to their surcoats, they were bound by strict rules. They ate in absolute silence, and were allowed meat and wine (well watered-down) three times per week. Knightly pastimes such as hawking were strictly forbidden.

From these humble beginnings, the order quickly developed until it became immensely wealthy and powerful, expanding into Western Europe and Britain. At its peak, the order ran over 50 estates or preceptories in England. The function of a preceptory was to raise revenue to support ongoing campaigns in the Holy Land and, as the equivalent of a charitable institution, it paid no taxes or tithes. Agriculture was an important source of funds, but it was soon discovered that money-lending generated a much greater income, and the Templars became as celebrated for their wealth as they had once been for their poverty.

A number of preceptories were established in Lincolnshire. The most significant (and one of the most important in the entire country) was that of Temple Bruer, situated mid-way between Lincoln and Sleaford. The Temple Bruer preceptory, enclosed by a

The surviving square tower of the church of the Knights Templar at Temple Bruer

moat or wall, was a thriving community and even had permission to hold a market. It would have included barns and a mill, workshops, a dairy and a brewery, accommodation and guesthouses. And, of course, there was a church – more precisely, one of the order's renowned 'round churches'.

Eventually, the Templars began to exploit their privileged position. For example, they were accustomed to holding Tournaments on their Temple Bruer estate, but these events created such a disturbance that they were banned by King Edward II. There were also long-running disputes with the neighbours, notably about the pasturage of livestock. And, on one occasion, the Preceptor of Temple Bruer was accused of extortion, having allegedly forced an individual to give him a sum of money to facilitate the purchase of a Roman coin he coveted.

Indeed, it was the Templars' wealth that led to their downfall. On 13th October 1307, in a series of dawn raids, all the Knights Templars in France were arrested by order of the king, Philip IV.

They faced a variety of charges, including heresy and blasphemy, undoubtedly manufactured by Philip as part of a scheme to confiscate the order's wealth. He succeeded in bullying Pope Clement V into abolishing the order (on 22nd March 1312) but failed in his principal objective, because the Templars' assets were handed over to another monastic-cum-military organisation: the Order of Knights Hospitallers.

In England, King Edward II followed Philip's example by seizing both the persons and property of the Templars. On 10th January 1308, the Preceptor of Temple Bruer, William de la More, and his knights were taken to Lincoln and faced a trial on 25th November 1309. Unlike many of Philip's victims, they did not end up being burned at the stake, but they did forfeit their property to the Crown – although, again, it was eventually given over to the Hospitallers, the original function of which had been to minister to sick and needy pilgrims to the Holy Land.

Like the Templars, the Hospitallers were no longer needed, for the Holy Land had effectively been lost in 1291. An attempt to retake it in 1300 had come to nothing, but the Hospitallers were not usurers, and avoided the fate of the Templars. Under their occupation, Temple Bruer lived on for another two centuries, before being swept away in the Dissolution of the Monasteries. Like many another ecclesiastical estate, it ended up in the possession of the Duke of Suffolk, who thereby gained some 2,000 acres of land. King Henry VIII is known to have visited Temple Bruer in 1541, en route to Lincoln, with his current queen, Catherine Howard and members of the Court, at which time, it was said, there were still 'great and vast buildings'.

The story of the estate thereafter is one of gradual decline and decay. By the mid-eighteenth century, the church had almost vanished. Archaeology has identified the course of the round nave of the church, which would have resembled the surviving examples at The Temple in London and St. Sepulchre's Church in Cambridge. In additional to a chancel, there were two towers, of which one – thanks to various twentieth century restoration projects – still exists. A rectangular, three-storey structure, 51 feet (15.5 metres) high, and dating from the early thirteenth century, it forms an unbroken link in a chain of 800 years of English history.

Peculiar Pillars

Lincolnshire has two celebrated high stone pillars. They are unusual in that both had a purpose and therefore neither can be classed as a folly.

Pelham's Pillar stands in Brocklesby Park, four miles to the south-west of Immingham. It was the brainchild of Charles Anderson-Pelham, 1st Earl of Yarborough. A celebrated yachtsman, he founded the Royal Yacht Squadron. When he died on board his own yacht in 1846, a monument in his memory was set up on Bembridge Downs on the Isle of Wight.

Anderson-Pelham was also a great planter of trees. Between 1727 and 1823, he planted a grand total of 12,552,700 trees on his property. In commemoration of this extraordinary feat, he built a stone pillar, 128 feet (39 metres) in height. The foundation stone was laid in 1840 and it was completed (at a cost of £2,400) in 1849, three years after his death. The entrance at the base was guarded by two stone lions, while a viewing tower at the top allowed the owner of the estate to survey his holdings.

Pelham Pillar's great rival, Dunston Pillar, lies alongside the A15, five miles to the south of Lincoln. The story of this stone column begins in the mid-eighteenth century when the land to the south of Lincoln comprised an expanse of desolate heath. Notorious as a haunt of highwaymen, the wilderness was a nightmare for travellers. A rudimentary road had been laid out in the 14th century, but time had rendered it obsolete, making it easy for folk to become disorientated, particularly on stormy winter evenings. Indeed, a number of lives had been lost.

The remains of the land lighthouse, built in 1751 by Sir Francis Dashwood as a guide for wayfarers

Among those who worried about crossing the heath at night was Sarah Ellis of nearby Nocton Hall. In 1742, Sarah married Sir Francis Dashwood, 15th Baron le Despencer of West Wycombe in Buckinghamshire. Dashwood is famous as a founder member of the 'Hellfire Club', but he also had a strong interest in social welfare. So impressed was he by his wife's fears that he devised a novel solution to the problem: he decided to build a land lighthouse.

The worthy project took a few years to reach fruition, but by 1751 the lighthouse was up and running. Contemporary likenesses show a structure very similar to the traditional offshore lighthouse. It was 92 feet (about 30 metres) in height and had an interior spiral staircase leading up to the base of an octagonal lantern, adding another 15 feet. From the top, on a clear day, the tower of St. Botolph's Church in Boston was visible 25 miles to the south-east. The lighthouse proved an invaluable point of reference for wayfarers, during both the hours of daylight and darkness. Soon, it became much more, for Sir Francis landscaped the immediate area in a scheme which even ran to the provision of a bowling green. In fact, it became one of Lincolnshire's earliest tourist attractions.

Sir Francis died in 1781. While the surrounds gradually fell into decay, the lighthouse functioned until 1788, by which time much of the heath had been enclosed and the road improved. The lantern was attacked by rust and in 1809, following a severe storm, it collapsed. The following year, the remains of the lantern casing were removed and the then-owner of Nocton Hall, Robert Hobart, 4th Earl of Buckingham, replaced it with a substantial statue of George III, to mark the king's 50-year reign.

The lighthouse pillar, with the statue on top, was only about a foot shorter than the original structure, but what had once been described as the 'Vauxhall' of Lincolnshire, in homage to the pleasure gardens situated on the south bank of the River Thames, had been reduced to a curiosity – or, as the diarist George Byng called it, an object of ridicule. Nevertheless, the pillar survived in its new form throughout the nineteenth century and almost halfway into the twentieth.

Its fate was sealed in 1939 when the Air Ministry decided to lay out an airfield at Coleby. It was literally across the road. A structure 91 feet high clearly constituted a danger to low flying aircraft, and drastic action needed to be taken. The statue was removed and the pillar's height reduced by 30 feet – leaving the stump we see today. The head and shoulders of George III's statue can be found in the grounds of Lincoln Castle, while a small wooden replica of the pillar adorns Dunston village green.

Julian's Bower

The village of Alkborough, which borders the River Trent, lies three miles to the north of Burton upon Stather. The Church of St. John the Baptist, given to Spalding Priory in 1052, was restored in the late nineteenth century by John Oldrid Scott, who designed the fine wooden porch. Etched into the stone floor of the porch is a small copy of a maze, the original of which – 'Julian's Bower' – stands a little to the south west, between the village and the river.

Julian's Bower does not conform to our usual concept of a maze. For example, it does not resemble the great maze at Hampton Court, which possesses a network of paths half a mile long, lined with seven foot-high yew/privet hedges. Julian's Bower is a turf maze. Instead of hedges, there is a single winding path of raised turf – a unicursal path, with no dead-ends, which leads to the centre. It has a diameter of about 40 feet (12 metres) with the turf paths cut to a depth of about six inches.

Some authorities argue that it should not be called a maze, but a labyrinth, although the words used to be largely interchangeable. The OED defines a maze as 'a confusing and baffling network of winding and intercommunicating paths' and a labyrinth as 'an intricate structure of intercommunicating passages through which it is difficult to find one's way without a clue'. Taken in this context, 'maze' would appear to be the more accurate term.

Many people are familiar with the classical tale of Theseus and the Minotaur. The Greek hero tracks the Minotaur, a creature half-man, half-bull, to its lair in a labyrinth at Knossos. Making his way through the labyrinth, he unwinds a ball of thread, so that when he has destroyed the Minotaur, he can find his way out. In this story, the labyrinth has a purpose, but what can be the function of a surface maze which is very easy to negotiate?

The concept of the maze was probably brought to Britain by the Romans. Julian's Bower is adjacent to the site of a Roman camp, known as 'Countess Close', and it was once thought that it was the focus of Roman games. Alternatively, it may have originated in the twelfth century with a small Benedictine monastic establishment, dependent upon Spalding Priory. A turf maze of this size might, indeed, be considered appropriate for introspective purposes. In addition, there are accounts of Akleborough villagers using it as a focal point for May-eve games, 'under an indefinite persuasion of something unseen and unknown co-operating with them'. This almost mystical quality is redolent of Shakespeare's reference to a turf maze in Act II, Scene 1 of *A Midsummer Night's Dream*, in which Titania states:

The nine men's morris is filled up with mud,
And the quaint mazes in the wanton green
For lack of tread are indistinguishable.

It is possible that, over time, usage has changed. Therefore, a turf maze may have begun life as a site for Roman games of one form or another and, much later, have been adapted or copied to fulfil a function connected with Christian worship. Later still, it could have played a role in seasonal festivals.

Turf mazes are very labour-intensive in terms of the on-going maintenance they require to keep them in good condition. Julian's Bower, for instance, has been re-cut many times and this explains why only a handful of British examples have survived. References

Julian's Bower, overlooking the south bank of the River Humber

are made to two more having existed in Lincolnshire, although there may have been several. There was a Julian's Bower (a common name for turf mazes) at Horncastle and another at Louth. The Louth site used to be indicated on Ordnance Survey maps as 'Julian Bower', although it has been impossible to determine its exact location. It was probably in the vicinity of the cemetery on London Road and the road called Julian Bower on the opposite side of London Road. In Thomas Allen's *History of the County of Lincoln*, published in 1833, the Horncastle site is identified as being 'near the junction of the two rivers on the south-west of the town', while the piece of land on which it stood 'retains the name of Julian Bower Close'.

Allen adds that the Julian Bower in Horncastle was used by youths for 'a martial game called Troy Town which, in after years, though divested of its martial character, continued to be amongst the healthy pastimes of the young'. Some turf mazes were called 'Troy Town' (as opposed to Julian's Bower) in connection with a Roman equestrian event which it is surmised may have been staged within their confines.

Whatever significance the turf mazes once undoubtedly had has long-since vanished. The handful of survivors, such as Alkborough, are now tourist attractions – and ones which certainly merit our attention.

Chapter Four

INTO BATTLE

The Battle of Lincoln, 2nd February 1141

King Henry I died in 1135. He had wanted his daughter, Matilda, to become queen, but many of the English barons looked askance at the prospect of swearing allegiance to a woman. An alternative candidate, Henry's nephew, Stephen of Blois, was more to their liking. Weak and pliable, unlike the strong-willed Matilda, he would, they quite rightly thought, be unable to exercise any control over them.

Stephen and Matilda were both abroad when Henry died, and Stephen reached London first, to be crowned king just three weeks after Henry's death. As expected, the barons ran riot, mercilessly exploiting the common people. And so began the period of English history known as 'The Anarchy', when, as Orderic Vitalis, writing in *Historiae Ecclesiasticae* reports, 'troubles spread everywhere far and wide and England was filled with plundering and burning and massacre.'

There was no shortage of support for Matilda, from the oppressed and from those barons who had not prospered under Stephen. One of the most dangerous enemies Stephen had made among such men was Ranulf, Earl of Chester. Shortly before Christmas 1140, Ranulf and William de Roumare seized Lincoln Castle – an important gain for Matilda's party. They approached the castle on pretence of making a friendly visit, sending their wives on ahead to allay any suspicion. Ranulf, accompanied by three

The East Gate, Lincoln Castle

knights followed. Once inside the castle, the small band grabbed whatever weapons they could find, overpowered the unsuspecting guards on duty and then opened the gates to admit their armed force.

They were not at leisure to enjoy their victory for long because. In the new year, Stephen arrived with an army of his own. He took and occupied the city by surprise during the hours of darkness and laid siege to the castle with the aid of catapults, siege engines and all the paraphernalia of early medieval siege warfare. Even so, Ranulf managed to slip away to raise a relief force. He appealed to the Earl of Gloucester – his father-in-law and Matilda's half-brother – who quickly assembled a force 1,000 strong, comprising his own retainers, a band of knights disinherited by Stephen and a contingent of Welsh mercenaries. By 1st February, they were approaching Lincoln.

Their appearance was a surprise to Stephen, who had ignored all warnings of their approach. The fording points of Fossdyke, the Roman canal connecting Lincoln with the River Trent, were inadequately guarded, enabling the earls to effect a crossing. Faced with a choice of withstanding a siege or making a stand, Stephen chose to fight, descending the following morning via Lincoln's West Gate. He arrayed his men – also numbering about 1,000 – in three divisions. On the left was the Flemish cavalry of William Ypres; on the right were several earls loyal to Stephen, and their mounted knights; in the middle were Stephen's men-at-arms and locally raised foot soldiers.

The precise rebel deployment is unclear, but the cavalry division of the Earl of Gloucester probably occupied the right wing, with the disinherited knights under de Roumare on the left and the infantry, including dismounted knights commanded by Ranulf, in the centre. The Welsh, lightly armed, were deployed on the flanks.

Stephen's earls, expecting the battle to open with a preliminary round of jousting, were shocked when de Roumare's knights attacked and immediately set to fighting at sword-point. Thoroughly discomfited, the earls retired, enabling de Roumare to turn in on Stephen's centre. For a time, it seemed that the balance might be redressed by Ypres, who charged forward to scatter the Welsh on the rebel right flank, before coming to grips with Gloucester's cavalry. With the aid of Ranulf's infantry, however, Ypres was checked. Thus deprived of its cavalry support, Stephen's infantry division was surrounded. Rebel cavalry and infantry closed in and the fighting spread into the streets of Lincoln. The king himself fought bravely, wielding a two-handed battle-axe and, when this broke, a sword. He was finally captured by a knight, William de Chesney, after being felled by a stone – perhaps a slingshot from one of the Welshmen. The victors sacked the city and slaughtered as many of its inhabitants as they could find.

Stephen himself was taken to Bristol Castle, to be confined in chains. Only the citizens of London and Stephen's queen kept his cause alive. Matilda was able to take what she considered to be her rightful place as Queen of England, but her triumph was destined to be short-lived, for her haughty demeanour began to turn the tide once more in Stephen's favour. In fact, Stephen's days of captivity were numbered for, in a further encounter between loyalists and rebels, at Winchester, the Earl of Gloucester was captured. An exchange of prisoners was arranged and Stephen gained his freedom, giving fresh impetus to the civil war that continued, unabated, until Stephen's own death in 1154.

The Battle of Losecoat Field, 12th March 1470

The year 1470 was a critical one in the lengthy civil conflict known as The Wars of the Roses, between the Houses of Lancaster and York. The Yorkist king, Edward IV, had a tenuous hold on the crown, but this was about to be challenged by a partnership of his own brother, George, Duke of Clarence and Richard Neville, Earl of Warwick – the latter, as 'The Kingmaker' having been largely responsible for placing Edward on the throne. Both Clarence and Warwick, dissatisfied with their degree of influence at Court, were plotting Edward's downfall, and thought they might attain their objective by exploiting unrest in Lincolnshire. Their scheme resulted in a battle which, although by no means the most important in Wars of the Roses annals, certainly bears the most curious name.

The Lincolnshire disturbances, which began in February 1470, were fronted by Richard, Lord Welles and his son, Sir Robert, assisted by Welles' brother-in-law, Sir Thomas Dymock. Welles, a relative of the Earl of Warwick, was based at Alford and could trace his ancestry back to the Norman Conquest. A relative newcomer to the Lincolnshire nobility was Sir Thomas Burgh of Gainsborough, a member of the King's Household. The Welles viewed him as an upstart and drove him out of the county.

An attack upon a member of the King's Household was a challenge to royal authority, and Edward sent for Welles and Dymock to explain themselves.

However, what had started as a family feud quickly developed into greater civil unrest, and Edward resolved to tackle it head-on by marching into Lincolnshire at the head of an army. Sir Robert

Welles, encouraged by Warwick, spread the word among the common people of Lincolnshire that the king intended to make an example of them, for they had been involved in dissension the previous year. Proclaiming himself the people's champion, Sir Robert raised a substantial armed force of his own. Apparently, Edward suspected no subterfuge, for he gave Warwick and Clarence permission to raise troops on his behalf. Their scheme was to join forces with Sir Robert, who would meet them at Leicester.

Edward left London on 7th March, progressing towards Lincolnshire via Royston and Huntingdon. By 11th March, he had reached Fotheringhay Castle. Warwick had told Sir Robert not to attempt to take on Edward alone but, worried about his father, he chose to ignore the planned rendezvous at Leicester and to stake all on a bold gamble.

On 12th March, the king, approaching Stamford from the south, discovered that he was on a collision course with Sir Robert, advancing from the north. Sir Robert expected Edward to rest in Stamford and although he hoped to make a decisive surprise attack, he stopped five miles short of the town, along a ridge of high ground slightly to the north of present-day Tickencote Warren.

Edward's response was to execute Lord Welles and Dymock, whom he had brought along with him, and to march out beyond Stamford to assault the potentially strong defensive position Sir Robert had selected. The highest contemporary estimate of the rebels' strength is 30,000 men, but the total was probably less than half this number. Edward's army may not have been larger, but it would have been better fed and armed.

Edward had a number of cannon – still something of a novelty on the battlefield – which were dragged laboriously up the Casterton road towards Tickencote. Progress must have been slow, with the rebels, now deployed squarely across the present-day A1, nervously observing the manoeuvres. As soon as the enemy was within range, the cannon were made ready and several salvos fired into the massed rebel ranks. They were probably inaccurate, causing minimal damage, but did succeed in giving the impression of superior strength.

In the confusion that the cannon fire created, the Yorkists launched an all-out assault on the enemy positions. That there was some resistance is proved by reported rebel cries of 'A Clarence! A Warwick!' designed to rally the troops, but as the Yorkist cavalry reached the ridge, all opposition collapsed. It is said that, in their haste to flee, the panic-stricken rebels cast away their jackets, this giving the battle its title. In the hope of escaping identification, it is, indeed, probable that Sir Robert's own retainers, who would have worn his livery, did throw away their coats. Others may have worn emblems, identifying them with the rebel host, and these would hurriedly have been torn from jackets and headgear. Even so, the slaughter of the rebels must have been great, many being cut down in a nearby wood which has retained the name 'Bloody Oaks'.

Sir Robert was subsequently captured, and executed a week later – but not before making a full confession in which he implicated Clarence and Warwick in the Lincolnshire rising. Edward denounced the pair as traitors and posted rewards for their capture. For the moment, it seemed that his victory at the Battle of Losecoat Field had established his authority as king. And a brief moment it would prove to be, for Clarence and Warwick succeeded in escaping to France, where they found Louis XI ready to aid and abet future schemes for reversing their fortunes.

The Battle of Gainsborough, 28th July 1643

Throughout the English Civil War between King Charles I and Parliament, the North Lincolnshire town of Gainsborough proved of interest to both sides. A crossing point of the River Trent, it also constituted an important part of the east midlands' road network.

Gainsborough, whose inhabitants, despite having Royalist sympathies, naively hoped to remain neutral, was first occupied in March 1643 by the Royalists. It proved to be a useful base for mounting raids into Parliamentarian country to the east, and Parliament's commander-in-chief in Lincolnshire, Francis, Lord Willoughby, was ordered to occupy it. On the night of 16th July, he launched a surprise attack and, after 'a desperate assault' took the town, securing the Royalist Earl of Kingston and 250 'common soldiers'. No sooner had Willoughby settled in, however, than he himself was besieged by Royalists, under the command of Sir Charles Cavendish – young cousin of the Earl of Newcastle – despatched from Newark. As Willoughby himself put it: 'The same day I took it, I was besieged before night'.

Parliament, in turn, organised a relief mission and, on 26 July, at Grantham, Sir John Meldrum joined forces with Colonel Oliver Cromwell, who had just taken Burghley House. An additional contingent of men from Lincoln ('Lincolneers') was collected the next day at North Scarle, bringing the total to around 1,200. After marching through the early hours of 28 July, the small army reached the village of Lea, two miles to the south of Gainsborough, where they encountered an advance party of Royalists.

After a sharp skirmish, the Royalists retreated to their main force, drawn up on Foxby Hill, to the east of the town. Although the Parliamentarians were outnumbered, they followed in what was a difficult ascent, for the ground was pitted with rabbit holes. Then, as they neared the summit, the pursuers came upon Cavendish and his main force. Cromwell remarks that the Royalists were 'well set' in two bodies, and that they charged downhill to try to take the Parliamentarians off-balance. Cromwell introduced his own cavalry, the ground being disputed for 'a pretty time' until the Royalists began to falter. Driving home their perceived advantage, the Parliamentarians chased them from the field in a pursuit which went on for five miles.

In an effort to turn the tide, Cavendish led a regiment he had held in reserve in an attack on the Lincolneers, who remained in the field and who were now thrown back in disarray. However,

Memorial plaque in an old stone gatepost, marks the site of the Battle of Gainsborough

Cromwell had held back three troops of Parliamentarian horse, with which he promptly took Cavendish in the flank. Cavendish and his men were chased down towards the River Trent. He himself either fell or was knocked from his horse in boggy ground before the river and despatched by a sword-thrust delivered by one of Cromwell's officers.

With the Royalists on the run, Gainsborough was hurriedly re-provisioned with powder and ammunition, but more Royalist troops were already reported to be approaching from the north. Accompanied by some 400 of Willoughby's infantry, the Parliamentarian horse led by Major Edward Whalley, went forth to meet them, thinking they would be mopping up survivors of Cavendish's force. They swept aside two troops of Royalist horse, encountered near Morton but, upon reaching high ground beyond the village, Whalley found himself looking down on the Earl of Newcastle's main army, 8,000 strong, which had advanced from Yorkshire.

When they were apprised of the situation, Willoughby and Cromwell agreed to withdraw the infantry and Cromwell left 'to bring them off'. He arrived on the scene to find the infantry being harried by Royalist cavalry and retreating 'in disorder'. Thanks to a brilliant rearguard action conducted by Whalley, most of the infantry were able to regain the relative safety of the town. Cromwell, his men and horses wearied, withdrew to Lincoln.

The Battle of Gainsborough is described by the renowned Civil War historian, Samuel Gardiner, as 'the turning point of the war'. Here, at last, was cavalry 'as highly disciplined as it was enterprising', with a commander who was 'prompt in action, sober in judgement, undaunted in the hour of adversity'. The battle also tells us something about Cromwell himself. Just three days later, on 31st July 1643, he was writing to the Committee of the Army of the Eastern Association to describe his great victory. He might have been censured for abandoning Gainsborough to its fate, when his brief had been to secure it for Parliament, but he argued – with justification – that there was little point in bottling up his cavalry inside the town. And so, Cromwell departed with the glory and Willoughby was left to carry the can.

In fairness, Cromwell did strongly urge the Association to send a substantial force to Gainsborough's relief, but the men could not be raised immediately, and so Willoughby had to shift for himself. The Earl of Newcastle bombarded the town with 16 pieces of artillery, setting buildings on fire. After three days, on 31st July – the same day on which Cromwell penned his self-congratulatory epistle – Willoughby surrendered, and Gainsborough was handed back to the Royalists.

'Winceby Fight', 11th October 1643

During the English Civil War (1642-1645) between King Charles I and Parliament, Lincolnshire's sympathies lay largely with Parliament. In September 1643, the county strengthened its hand by joining Parliament's Eastern Association of counties, although it still remained vulnerable to attack from the Royalist stronghold of Newark in the west. At this time, the walled city of Lincoln, which frequently changed hands, was held by the Royalists who also occupied Bolingbroke Castle. It was the Army of the Eastern Assocation's attempt to take the castle that presaged the Battle of Winceby or 'Winceby Fight'.

The Army's commander, the Earl of Manchester, laid siege to Bolingbroke on 9th October 1643. On the same day, a Parliamentarian detachment at Horncastle was surprised by Sir John Henderson, Royalist Governor of Newark, who had cobbled together an army of some 3,000 men to stem the Parliamentarian advance into the heart of the county. Leaving an adequate force to continue the siege, Manchester marched towards Horncastle to meet Henderson. The two sides clashed five miles to the east of Horncastle at the hamlet of Winceby.

On 11th October, Royalists and Parliamentarians drew up on ridges about half a mile apart. In the middle was open ground, dipping slightly. For the Parliamentarians – probably under 3,000 strong – Manchester organised a vanguard, comprising his own and Lieutenant General Oliver Cromwell's regiments of Horse, supported by the regiment of Sir Thomas Fairfax in the rear. The infantry had not yet arrived and Manchester hurried back to chase them up. The Royalists deployed in four divisions: Henderson's regiment of Horse on the left, Sir William Savile's Horse in the centre and on the right, and one division, probably with the

The ruins of the Curtain Wall of Bolingbroke Castle. The Parliamentarian attempt to secure the castle led to the Civil War encounter at Winceby

addition of infantry, in the rear. Both sides were fronted by a body of dragoons known as a 'Forlorn Hope', the function of which was to open hostilities.

In fact, the opposing sides faced each other for about an hour before the Forlorn Hopes dismounted and began firing into the enemy. The cavalry began descending the slopes from either ridge and, as Cromwell reached the plain, his horse was shot from beneath him. Scrambling to his feet, he was promptly knocked down by a Royalist, Sir Ingram Hopton. Had Hopton despatched Cromwell there and then, he would have changed the course of history. Acting from a sense of honour, however, he attempted to make Cromwell his prisoner. In so doing, he was himself shot and killed, allowing the Lieutenant General to commandeer a trooper's mount and rejoin the fighting.

Initially, Henderson's cavalry held their own against Cromwell. Then Fairfax, swinging around from the rear, attacked Savile's right flank. Savile's Horse were ordered to 'Face About' to meet Fairfax head-on, but this instruction seems to have been misinterpreted and some of the men turned their mounts aside, as if to retreat. As often happened in battle, the retiring front line quickly caused chaos in the rear. On the other side of the battle-field, Cromwell finally overcame Henderson's resistance and the Royalists here also turned tail.

Many of Henderson's men came to grief in the marshes of Snipe Dale. The Royalist centre and left were even less fortunate. Retreating along the lane ('Slash Lane') they were cut down mercilessly by Fairfax's Horse. The dragoons who had lost their mounts tried to escape by fleeing across country ('Slash Hollow') but they came up against a hedge with a gate which opened towards them. Such was the pressure of men that it could not be opened and they became easy prey for their pursuers. Manchester's infantry had now arrived and joined in the slaughter. Eventually, Manchester succeeded in bringing an end to the carnage. When it was all over, Royalist dead and wounded numbered in the region of 1,000 with a further 1,000 taken prisoner, while the Parliamentarians claimed losses of only twenty killed and sixty wounded.

Parliament made much of the victory, and it is true that gains were made. In the absence of a strong, mobile Royalist force, both Lincoln and Bolingbroke Castle fell to Manchester's army. Repercussions were also felt in Yorkshire, where the Royalist Earl of Newcastle was laying siege to Hull. On the same day as the Battle of Winceby was fought, the Hull garrison (commanded by Lord Fairfax, Sir Thomas's father) made a successful assault on the siege works. When Newcastle received news of Henderson's defeat, he feared that Manchester would be able to advance through Lincolnshire to threaten his flank, so he decided to raise the siege and fall back on York for the winter.

While relatively minor encounters such as Winceby had little national importance, they were often significant in paving the way for the large, set-piece battles to come, such as Marston Moor (1644) and Naseby (1645), that would determine the outcome of the English Civil War.

Chapter Five

CRIME & PUNISHMENT

The Murder of William Storr

Seventeenth century Lincolnshire was the scene of many disputes over the enclosure of common land. One such altercation occurred in 1602, in the town of Market Rasen and led, indirectly, to the murder of a clergyman, the Reverend William Storr. It is of particular interest because the case was well documented in a pamphlet first published in 1603.

At issue in this particular case were the rights of Market Rasen's inhabitants 'concerning their Commons and Liberty in the town fields', which the 'Lords' of the town wanted to limit. Tempers boiled over one Sunday 'about Lammas Day' in the Church of St Thomas, when the evening service, conducted by the Reverend Storr, ended. An unruly argument broke out between the respective parties, and Storr tried to restore order. He suggested that both sides nominate representatives to speak for them. This was agreed upon and Storr was asked to mediate. He did so unwillingly, coming out against the Lords and in favour of the 'free-holders and the rest of the Commons'.

Among the congregation was Francis Cartwright, son of one of the Lords and a young man of 'unbridled humour'. He criticised Storr who, having experience of the young man's 'hot stomach and hastiness' tried to ignore him. This provoked Francis into launching into an abusive tirade comprising much 'base and odious' language.

The next day, Storr and others approached the elder Cartwright to tackle him about his son's reprehensible behaviour. Francis interrupted the discussion, and 'continued as the night before' with his unbridled abuse of the clergyman. Only with difficulty did his father prevent him from attacking Storr with a dagger. Francis stormed off to the Market Place, where he denounced his perceived enemy as a 'scurvy, lousy, paltry Priest'. Now thoroughly alarmed, Storr sought the protection of the law, requesting that Francis be bound over to be of good behaviour, but the matter was deferred until the next Quarter Sessions.

On the following Sunday, in church, Storr based his sermon on Isaiah, Chapter I, Verse 9: *Except the Lord of hosts had left unto us a very small remnant, we should have been as Sodom and we should have been like unto Gomorrah.* Francis took this as a personal admonishment, as a result of which he 'more and more thirsted for revenge'. (One might express surprise that he went to church at all, but attendance was compulsory, with fines levied on absentees.)

Matters came to a head on the morning of 30 August, when Francis saw Storr walking alone on the south side of the town. Immediately, he went into a cutler's, emerging a short time later with a well-honed sword. Hurrying after Storr, he drew the weapon and set about him. With his first blow, he all but severed the clergyman's left leg, following up with two heavy blows to the head. Storr, who was unarmed, fell to the ground and Francis continued his frenzied attack, until the cries of an approaching woman caused him to flee. (Later, he would claim that he had only intended to inflict 'some slight wounding' on his victim.) More people appeared and Storr was carried to the nearest house where, for three hours, surgeons laboured to save him. For a week, he hovered between life and death, before finally succumbing to his dreadful wounds.

Francis, meanwhile, had made for his father's home, where he was arrested by constables and hauled before a Justice of the Peace. Instead of being kept in custody, however, he was bailed on the surety of a nominal sum – an act for which the JP was later suspended. Not surprisingly, Francis used the opportunity to abscond. Initially, he tried to reach Scotland, but was captured and imprisoned at Berwick. Managing to escape, he returned south and is next heard of in Warwick where he was questioned on suspicion of robbery. Eventually, he made his way to France and then to Holland, where he remained until the following year when, despite the barbarity of the crime, his father contrived to secure a Pardon for him – a decision that was challenged, unsuccessfully, by Storr's widow – and the fugitive was able to return home.

One might have expected this miraculous escape from justice (coupled with his subsequent marriage) to have curbed Francis's rashness but it didn't, for he killed again. This time, he assaulted and fatally injured a man called Riggs in Grantham. Apprehended before he could run, he was put on trial for murder. The luck of the Devil remained with him, for he was found guilty only of manslaughter and sentenced to one year's imprisonment. Upon his release, he continued in his wild ways and was, at length, driven by spiralling debt to join the navy, sailing under Sir Richard Hawkins in an expedition to reduce the Algerian corsairs. Even here, he could not keep out of trouble and was cashiered following numerous altercations with his shipmates.

Shortly thereafter, he published a memoir entitled *The Life, Confession and Heartie Repentance of Francis Cartwright* – an outpouring of sanctimonious nonsense in which he lays the blame for his crimes squarely upon the shoulders of his victims. Storr, he argues, could have avoided his fate by using 'greater words and milder reprehensions', while Riggs was 'a man urged by his own rashness to seek his own fall by my hand.' Similarly, his problems in the navy were entirely due to everyone else, and their 'secret heart-burnings against me.' While his further exploits are not recorded, his state of mind was such that today he would almost certainly have been detained 'at Her Majesty's Pleasure', in an appropriate institution.

Tom Otter's Gibbet

On 3rd November 1805, at the church of St Michael & All Angels in South Hykeham, Lincolnshire, a 'knobstick wedding' took place between Thomas Temporal and Mary Kirkham. The groom, a 23-year-old canal navvy (or 'banker' to use the Lincolnshire term), had fallen foul of the 1732 Bastardy Act, for Mary was heavily pregnant. Under the terms of this legislation, a man could be gaoled until such time as he provided for the maintenance of an illegitimate child. The alternative was a forced marriage, the term 'knobstick' referring to the stave of office carried by a church warden, who often supervised the ceremony.

The bride did not know that her lover was using his mother's maiden name as an alias. His real name was Thomas Otter, and he already had a wife. The previous year, in what was almost certainly another compulsory ceremony, he had married Martha Rawlinson at Eakring, Nottinghamshire. Shortly afterwards, a daughter had been born. Thus, Mary constituted something of an inconvenience, but Otter was not too worried because he had a plan to deal with it.

Later in the day, the newlyweds were sighted eight miles away, in the vicinity of Saxilby, walking towards Drinsey Nook, a tract of lonely moor which Otter probably knew well, having been born and raised in the nearby Nottinghamshire village of Treswell. Exactly what happened next will never be known, but the next morning, two men stumbled upon Mary's battered body lying in what would become known as Tom Otter's Lane. It was taken to the Sun Inn at Saxilby, together with what appeared to be the murder weapon: a bloodstained hedge-stake. The inquest into her death returned a verdict of wilful murder against her husband. He was subsequently arrested in Lincoln and held in the goal within Lincoln Castle, where he languished until his trial at the Lent Assizes, on 12th March 1806.

The court records have not survived, but we do know that the trial lasted five hours and that twenty witnesses were called for the prosecution. The evidence was purely circumstantial in that no one had actually seen the murder take place, yet the 'Guilty' verdict came as no surprise. The judge, Sir Robert Graham, pronounced sentence of death. Initially, he decreed that the body should be consigned to the dissecting table, and the condemned man must have thought that nothing could be worse. If so, he was wrong, for Graham subsequently changed his mind. Instead, the remains would be hung in chains (or 'gibbeted') near the scene of the crime – a fate intended to act as a deterrent and usually reserved for career criminals such as highwaymen.

Otter was allowed only two days to prepare himself for death. At dawn on 14th March 1806, he was taken out to the gallows in Westgate to be hanged before an enthusiastic audience. Afterwards, the body was returned to the castle to await completion of the gibbeting irons. On the morning of 20th March, all was ready and a cart, accompanied by a mob of spectators, set out for

Tom Otter's Lane, where Tom Otter's body was hung in chains. As one looks at the photograph, the gibbet (marked on the 1824 Ordnance Survey map) was situated on the right of the road - now the B1190

Drinsey Nook. At a point midway along Tom Otter's Lane, a high gallows with a projecting arm at the top was erected and the ghastly exhibit hoisted up. The Reverend George Hall ('The Gypsy's Parson' – see page 101) recalled his own grandfather's description of the party atmosphere. 'For several days after the event,' wrote Hall, 'the vicinity of the gibbet resembled a country fair with drinking booths, ballad singers, Gipsy fiddlers and fortune tellers.' Thereafter, bands of gypsies often camped at the spot, which they knew to be studiously avoided by locals after dark. The only other regular visitors were birds, the *Magazine for Natural History* of 1832 reporting that a pair of tits had successfully nested in the remains of the corpse's mouth – giving rise to the following rhyme:

> *There were ten tongues all in one head*
> *The tenth went out to fetch some bread*
> *To feed the living in the dead.*

One would have thought this tale sufficiently gruesome to satisfy the most macabre mind and yet, over the years, additional gratuitous grisly details have been appended. Although entirely fictitious, they have become accepted as fact. Several originated in an article by Thomas Miller that appeared in *The Lincolnshire Times* of 22nd November 1859. According to Miller, the mounting steps of the *Sun Inn* were stained with the victim's blood 'that neither sand nor freestone, nor all the scrubbing in the world would ever remove'. Miller also claimed that for many years afterwards, on 3rd November, the cry of a new born child could be heard in the room where Mary's body had been placed. In addition, on the same night, the murder weapon, originally stored at the *Sun Inn* would be mysteriously transported to the scene of the crime.

Tom Otter holds the distinction of being the last person in Lincolnshire to be gibbeted. His gibbet survived until 1850, when it was blown down in a storm. Not surprisingly, perhaps, the *Sun Inn*, now allegedly haunted by the spirit of Otter himself, has become a place of pilgrimage for ghost-hunters.

The Executioner

On 1st April 1872, William Horry was executed in Lincoln. The condemned man, an alcoholic publican who had shot dead his wife, was the first person to be hanged by William Marwood. From that time, until his own death in 1883, Marwood hanged a further one hundred and seventy one men and eight women.

To the modern mind, there is something positively ghoulish about anyone who would aspire to be a public executioner. And yet, Marwood, a cobbler who kept a shop in Church Lane, Horncastle lobbied fiercely for the job. He spent much time practising on pigs and sheep, and was even permitted to use the gallows in Lincoln gaol for his experiments. The governor, impressed by his diligence, decided to try him out on Horry. Observers noted that the execution was quick and clean, unlike many of those performed by William Calcraft, whom Marwood soon replaced as 'Number One'.

Calcraft (also a cobbler by trade), used the 'short drop' method of hanging, in which the victim, noose about his neck, stood on a low cart. When the cart moved away, he was left dangling in mid-air and slowly strangled to death. An improvement was made from 1866, with the introduction of the 'standard drop' which allowed for a fall of up to six feet. Marwood refined the practice in his development of the 'long drop', by which a person's build was taken into account in determining the extent of the fall required to ensure that the neck was broken and death instantaneous. He went on to devise a table comprising a list of body weights and corresponding lengths of rope, which was used as a source of reference by hangmen until the abolition of capital punishment in 1969.

Initially, Marwood tried to keep his activities a secret. However, five of his executions were performed in his home county where there was always a chance that he would be recognised. This happened when he went to Lincoln in August 1875, to hang

Peter Blanchard, who had knifed a girl for rejecting his advances. A neighbour of Marwood's discovered why he was there and the news soon spread through Horncastle. It is said that even Marwood's wife did not know about his part-time job, although, by the time he got to Blanchard, he had already performed 28 executions throughout the length and breadth of the country. In any event, when word got around, he was shunned by Horncastle folk.

The population at large was not so fussy, and Marwood quickly became a magnet for the morbidly curious who flocked to his shop for a sight of the hangman. They paid over the odds for his shoemaking services and were sometimes treated to a sixpenny tour of memorabilia he collected in the course of his official engagements. These fringe benefits, in addition to the £10 (plus expenses) he received for each hanging, made him a rich man.

Marwood was a great believer in capital punishment, arguing that there was 'no better deterrent than hanging', yet he thought that every condemned man, regardless of his crime, had a right to die as painlessly as possible. Celebrated criminals to benefit from this progressive philosophy included Henry Wainwright, who killed and dismembered his lover; physician and poisoner George Henry Lamson, and the perpetrators of the 'Phoenix Park Murders' of Lord Frederick Cavendish and Thomas Henry Burke. It is also worthy of note that Marwood carried out one public execution. The last public execution in England had taken place in 1868, but Marwood's travels took him to Jersey, where public executions were not outlawed until 1907. Thus, on 11th August 1875, he hanged Joseph Le Brun (convicted of killing his own sister) in front of a large crowd outside the Newgate Street gaol in St. Helier.

Although a tremendous improvement upon previous practice, Marwood's system was not fool-proof and, inevitably, there were occasions when things did not go according to plan. At Durham gaol, on 6th August 1883, what should have been a routine job went badly wrong, with the subject, James Burton, somehow getting entangled in the rope when the trap door opened. He had to be hoisted up and dropped again. The newspapers produced hostile accounts of the episode and a question was asked in the House of Commons by Joseph Cowen, MP for Newcastle-upon-Tyne, while the Member for County Sligo, Thomas Sexton, drew attention to another case: that of Miles Joyce, hanged by Marwood in Galway on 15th December 1882. Here again, the rope had to be disentangled. According to press reports, Marwood had been reduced to pushing Joyce down by the shoulders – a stratagem often resorted to by Calcraft.

The upshot was that Marwood was suspended from his duties. His death, following a short illness four weeks later, spared him any further ignominy. It was a sad end for the Lincolnshire man who had succeeded in introducing an element of humanity into the terrible pronouncement: *'...and there be hanged by the neck until you shall be dead.'*

Until 1859, public executions were carried out on the flat roof of Cobb Tower, on the north-east corner of Lincoln Castle. Prior to a hanging, merrymakers would gather beneath the castle walls, at the appropriately named 'The Strugglers Inn'

Chapter Six

CURIOUS CUSTOMS

The Stamford Bull Run

Bull running is essentially a Spanish pastime. The most celebrated event takes place in the city of Pamplona. Half a dozen bulls and several steers are released onto the streets of a cordoned-off section of the city. As they run through the streets, they are preceded by people who try to outrun them. This often results in the runners sustaining injuries that require hospital treatment. It is said that the practice originated in the fourteenth century, when cattle were being driven from the fields to the towns. In an effort to speed-up the process, the beasts would be goaded into a gallop.

It is interesting to learn that the recreation was once popular in Britain, although only in two locations: the Staffordshire town of Tutbury and Stamford in Lincolnshire. But there was one important difference: the runners usually stayed behind the bull. The Tutbury bull runs originated in the fourteenth century with John of Gaunt, ruler of England during the minority of his nephew, King Richard II. In 1371, John married Constance, daughter of King Peter of Castile. Tetbury Castle was one of the couple's favourite residences, and John introduced bull running through the town's thoroughfares to make his wife feel more at home.

The Stamford bull runs predate those of Tutbury and can be traced back to 1209. At that time, William de Warenne, owner of the estate of Stamford, saw a bull running wild in the town, where it gored a number of people. He chased after it on horseback and enjoyed the experience so much that he arranged for a bull to be released into the streets every year.

Bull running should not be confused with bull-baiting (although, as will be seen, the two practices were sometimes organised in tandem.) Bull baiting involved tethering a bull to a stake so that it could be 'baited' by dogs which, as time went on, were specially bred for the purpose – hence the bulldog breed. It was often argued that the baiting of a bull prior to butchering, actually improved the quality of the meat.

In Tutbury, minstrels played a leading role in the proceedings, chasing the bull following attendance at a church service and banquet. The annual Stamford bull run, which took place on 13th November, was more democratic. Tradesmen would shut up shop and the bull would be released into the streets, to be chased by men, women and children. It could prove difficult to encourage the bull to run. It might be cudgelled, have its tail cut off, prodded with sharp sticks, shot at or have pepper thrown in its face. Thus the creature was nearly driven mad with fear and pain. And it seems to have been the people who would chase the bull, as opposed to an enraged bull chasing the people. When the bull was exhausted and could go no further, it would be dragged back through the town to be tied up and baited before being killed.

The annual bull running day gradually acquired much ceremonial baggage. An integral part of the festivities had always consisted of the participants throwing mud at one another, but more civilised elements were introduced. For example, a 'bull queen' was appointed to preside over the affairs, and the 'bullards' themselves, as the bull chasers came to be known, began to sport colourful costumes.

It has been argued that during the eighteenth century, bull running became very much a working class pastime. Certainly, the accompanying pageantry declined as unauthorised single-street bull runs began to be organised on days other than 13th November.

They were the eighteenth century equivalents of today's illegal car races, and a number of serious injuries resulted, not least because many of the participants were often drunk.

The nineteenth century saw the birth of the animals rights movement. The first piece of animal welfare legislation, aimed at the welfare of cattle, appeared in 1822, and The Society for the Prevention of Cruelty to Animals (which would develop into the RSPCA) was founded in 1824. It was not until 1835, however, that the Cruelty to Animals Act (Pease's Act) extended the legislation to cover bulls, dogs, bears, goats and sheep. The early efforts of the SPCA to stop bull running angered the folk of Tutbury and Stamford, and bull runs continued to be held, despite the authorities' efforts to stop them – which included calling in the army. It may even be the case that the pressure to suppress bull running did much to extend its life. When the SPCA sent activists up to Stamford from London, they were thrown out of the town. However, unlike the twentieth-century campaign against fox-hunting – a national recreation – bull running, with only two functioning centres, was an easy target for the protestors and finally succumbed to changing attitudes.

Bull running in Stamford has been revived, of late, as part of the town's Georgian Festival. Amid a carnival atmosphere, a festooned bull, roughly modelled from wood, is pushed on castors through the streets. A woman (presumably the bull queen) rides on top of the bull, which is followed by the bullards or, in this case, costumed street performers. It is all enacted with the best of intentions but, somehow, it just isn't the same.

The Haxey Hood

Haxey, described by Edwardian author and journalist Arthur Mee as a 'pleasant little market town' lies in Isle of Axholme territory, just inside the Lincolnshire border and 12 miles to the east of Doncaster. It has a acquired some celebrity for a ritualistic rough-and-tumble game called 'The Haxey Hood', which takes place annually on 'Twelfth Night'.

According to legend, the game has its origins in the fourteenth century. On a particular twelfth night, as the lady of the manor of Haxey, Lady de Mowbray, was riding over Haxey Hill, the wind caught hold of her hood and swept it away. A group of thirteen local peasants, working in the fields, ran after it. The man who retrieved it was too shy to return it and gave it to one of the others to hand it back to Lady de Mowbray, who was so tickled by the incident that she promised to make a grant of land to the men if they would re-enact the pantomime each year on 6th January. She dubbed the man who caught her hood, 'the Fool', the one who returned it, 'The Lord' and the rest of the men, 'Boggins' – a word of Scottish origin, meaning grotesquely ugly and smelly.

This practice eventually developed into The Haxey Hood game. Over time, the Boggins became officials who presided over an event in which members of the public were the participants. Lady de Mowbray's hood was symbolised by a cylindrical object – either a rolled up sack or a leather tube, about two feet in length and between two and four inches wide. The latter was stuffed with straw (or, on one recorded instance during the 1950s, money – namely twelve threepenny pieces and one half-sovereign). The Fool, his face smeared with soot, was bedecked in strips of coloured cloth and the Boggins dressed in red smocks.

In mid-Victorian times, for a week or so, over the Christmas period, the Boggins, accompanied by the Fool, visited every dwelling in the neighbourhood, singing songs and asking for money to purchase a leather Hood, made by a saddler. Early in the afternoon of 6th January, The Fool would stand on the base of an old stone cross near the Church of St. Nicholas and give a speech of welcome to the assembled crowds, concluding with the words: *Hoose against hoose, toon against toon. And if you meet a man knock him doon.* Then, everyone repaired to a field behind the church. In what was a preliminary event, The Lord threw one of several Hoods made of sacking into the air and the man who caught it would try to make off with it – either supported by his friends or opposed by the rest. If a Boggin managed to get hold of it, then it was returned to the Lord.

Finally, late in the afternoon, the leather 'Sway Hood' was thrown up. What followed resembled a game of rugby football, with the Hood being moved, in part, by individuals running with it, and at other times being carried along in a scrum or 'sway'. At length, it finished up at the door of a particular public house, the man who delivered it receiving a cash

The Mowbray Stone, in front of the Church of St. Nicholas, starting point for the Haxey Hood game

prize. The following day, the Fool would be 'smoked', a process that involved tying a rope around his waist and dangling him over a fire made up of damp straw.

A number of subtle changes have been made to suit the 21st century. The Fool and the Boggins still do their seasonal visiting, but the money they collect is now given to local voluntary organisations. On Twelfth Night, the Fool opens the proceedings a little later than used to be the case, because the leading characters spend the early afternoon on a ceremonial pub crawl through Haxey and Westwoodside. Nowadays, the Fool is smoked immediately after he has given his welcoming speech. The smoking process is far less demanding, for the subject merely stands in front of a pile of damp straw – although there have still been occasions within

living memory when the Fool, standing too close to the conflagra-
tion, has caught fire.

The 'officials' and the would-be participants make their way
to the pitch. The Fool appears to have retained his regalia, but
the Lord now wears a coat of hunting pink, as does the 'Chief
Boggin' – a relatively recently created post. The rest of the Boggins
wear red sweaters. The preliminary event, in which the Hood is
thrown up into the air, has become a game for children, who chase
a number of Sack Hoods. The main game gets underway when
the Sway Hood is thrown. It is moved only by a swaying process
within a giant scrum. The scrum, which can involve hundreds of
players, sways about for hours on end until the Hood is manoeu-
vred towards one of four public houses – currently The Carpenter's
Arms, Duke William Hotel, King's Arms, The Loco.

One cannot help but notice the resemblance between the
Haxey Hood game and Stamford Bull Running (see page 56).
The stories of the origins of both customs are not dissimilar and
both are constructed around an activity in which everyone can get
involved, thereby engendering a sense of community. Also, long
ago, it may have been the practice to use the head of a bull as the
Hood. If so, then the roasting of the remainder of the beast would
have formed a suitable conclusion for the festivities.

Ecclesiastical Customs

The village of Glentham lies on the A631, 2½ miles to the east
of Caenby Corner. Adjoining Glentham is the hamlet of Caenby
(originally Cavenby), once home to the de Tourney family.
A number of monuments to the de Tourneys are to be found
in Glentham's Church of St. Peter & St. Paul. The church was
originally dedicated to Our Lady of Sorrows, a reminder of which
is to be seen in a sculpture of the Virgin Mary cradling the body of
Jesus. Herein, strangely enough, lies the origins of the local custom
known as 'Washing Molly Grime'.

It all began with the ceremonial practice of the washing, by several virgins, of an effigy of the dead Christ every Good Friday, and the strewing of his bier with flowers prior to a re-enacted entombment.

The water used for the ritual was obtained from Newel's Well, 1½ miles to the west, and would be carried, in procession, up the hill to the village. The well itself is not a 'Holy Well', although one comes across the occasional vague tale concerning the healing powers of its waters. In all probability, the connection arose from the nature of the ritual itself.

At some stage, the ceremony underwent a radical transformation, with the holy image being replaced by that of a brass effigy of one of the de Tourneys – supposedly that of Lady Anne Tourney, who lived in the fourteenth century. The work came to be carried out by seven 'old maids' who were paid a shilling each out of an annual rent charge on a parcel of local land. Over time, the effigy became worn and mutilated, acquiring the name 'Molly Grime' – possibly a corruption of *malgraen*, an old word referring to the washing of holy images.

The ceremony ceased around 1832, when the land was sold and the rent charge lost. Some accounts identify the owner of the land at that time as 'W. Thorpe'. In fact, his name was William Thorpe and financial problems led to the sale of his property. The record of bankruptcy proceedings against him – convened to 'make a dividend of his estate and effects' – gives his profession as 'farmer, dealer and chapman', suggesting that he eked out a living as best he could. Thorpe died in 1836, at the age of 56. According to parish records, he died from natural causes 'occasioned by his extreme depression of mind proceeding from his misfortunes'.

It may be thought unusual that, given the present-day fashion for the revival of ancient customs, 'Washing Molly Grime' has not been resurrected. Apparently, a variation reappeared briefly under the guise of 'The Molly Grime Run', but its ultimate abandonment is probably due to the fact that Newel's Well appears to have run

The Caistor Gad Whip, kept in Caistor's Church of St. Peter & St. Paul

dry. Not only the ritual but also the water supply has run its course.

A positively bizarre custom, which ceased shortly after the custom of 'Washing Molly Grime', used to take place in the Church of St. Peter and St. Paul in Caistor. It involved what is known as 'The Caistor Gad Whip'.

Every Palm Sunday, a man from the village of Raventhorpe, near present-day Scunthorpe, took a whip to St. Peter & St. Paul's Church. The stock of the instrument was made of ash and wrapped in four pieces of wych-elm. A 'gad' was an old linear measurement, equivalent to nine feet. Hence, the thong, also of white leather, was about nine feet in length. At the commencement of the 1st lesson of the day, the whip was cracked three times in the porch. The man then tied a purse containing two shillings to the top of the stock, entered the church and stood in front of the reading desk until the 2nd lesson was begun. He waved the whip and purse over the minister's head before kneeling down and keeping the whip suspended over him until the lesson was ended. After the service, the whip was carried to the manor house at Hundon, where it resided until the following year.

Accounts of the ritual do vary slightly. The money in the purse is usually said to have comprised 24 silver pennies, although 30 silver pennies are occasionally mentioned, perhaps in allusion to the 30 pieces of silver which Judas Iscariot received for betraying Jesus. The whip is sometimes described as being deposited in the pew belonging to the Lord of the Manor of Hundon, and a new whip may have been used each year.

The origin of the ritual is unknown. One story involves an argument between the Lords of the Manors of Hundon and Broughton over a parcel of land. They settled the matter by engaging in single-combat. Although the Lord of the Manor of Hundon prevailed, he agreed to cede the land on condition that the ritual should be performed annually.

In 1836, the Lord of the Manor of Hundon petitioned Parliament to ban the ceremony, describing it as superstitious and 'utterly inconsistent with a place of a Christian worship'. He also offered to guarantee the churchwardens against any loss, implying that, somewhere along the line, money – perhaps the 24 silver pennies – changed hands. The petition was unsuccessful, for the ceremony continued until 1846. Today, the gad-whip, as last used, is kept in a glass case inside the church.

Chapter Seven

ENTERTAINERS

Buffalo Bill Comes to Town

Whenever one thinks of the old American West, the one name which invariably comes to mind is that of William Frederick 'Buffalo Bill' Cody. In many ways, Cody *was* the old West. He rode for the Pony Express, scouted for the army, fought the Sioux and Cheyenne, worked as a buffalo hunter – killing over 4,000 of the beasts in a period of eighteen months – and, in later life, ran the greatest show on earth.

Cody began his theatrical career in 1872, when he was just 26 years old, starring with his friend, James Butler 'Wild Bill' Hickok, in a play produced by Ned Buntline. In 1876, while on scouting duties, Cody killed and scalped a Cheyenne chief, Yellow Hand – an incident which was included in his subsequent stage performances. It began to dawn on him that when it came to action sequences, the theatre had its limitations. And so, in 1883, he formed 'Buffalo Bill's Wild West' show.

Cody's aim was to depict the old western way of life in a series of snapshots. The extravaganza (for it was far more than a 'show') involved a one-thousand-strong cast performing feats of horsemanship with demonstrations of sharp-shooting and the re-enactment of historical scenes, such as The Battle of Little Big Horn. Participants included the Sioux chief, Sitting Bull, sharp-shooter Annie Oakley and frontierswoman Jane 'Calamity Jane' Cannary. It was an immediate success, in part because it presented the old west in ways people wanted to remember it. With Cody, fact and fiction were always inseparable.

In addition to travelling throughout the United States, the show made several forays into Europe. In 1887, it visited England for the American Exhibition, giving a Royal Command Performance for Queen Victoria.

In 1891, a tour was made of the larger English cities, including Liverpool, Birmingham, Manchester and Leeds, but it was not until 1903 and 1904 that the show's major UK tours took place.

By this time, the show was past its very best. From the beginning, Sitting Bull had refused to tour Europe. In 1890, he was killed by Indian police at Standing Rock Reservation. Annie Oakley was seriously injured in a railroad accident in 1901 and Calamity Jane was fired in 1902 for disruptive behaviour. Furthermore, Cody himself was not a good businessman. Money was still coming in, but it was also going out, and his expenses were prolific.

All the same, the 1903 season saw British audiences, including those in Boston, Grantham, Lincoln and Spalding captivated by the wild west spectacle. On 23rd September, two performances, at 2.00pm and 8.00pm, were given in Spalding. A large arena, capable of accommodating 200 horses at any one time, was set up in Green Waltham's Park on Pinchbeck Road. Some 15,000 visitors thrilled at the sight of Buffalo Bill, described as 'a fine picturesque figure ... straight as a lance'. Re-enactments included an Indian attack on the Deadwood stage and a new item: the capture of San Juan Hill by Teddy Roosevelt's Rough Riders during the Spanish-American War of 1898. It was Cody who coined the term 'rough riders'. In fact, since 1893, the show had been called 'Buffalo Bill's Wild West & Congress of Rough Riders of the World'. Roosevelt had called his unit 'The Rough Riders' as a tribute to the frontiersman.

In the early hours of the following morning, the show left for Boston, where it performed before an estimated 17,000 people. On 25th September, it moved on to Grantham and then Lincoln on 26th September. To describe the schedule as gruelling would be an understatement, the 1903 British tour alone taking in over 90 provincial towns and cities from Aberdeen to Penzance.

The final tour of Britain took place in 1904 and included dates at two Lincolnshire venues: Gainsborough (at Highfield Grange) on 29th June and Grimsby on 30th June, where the show arrived on five trains between 2.00am and 3.00am. It appears that after packing up following performances in one town, the troupe would grab a few hours sleep while in transit to the next. Thus, by 5.00am, everyone was up and about making preparations for the Grimsby show. A makeshift camp was set up on Clee Road in Cleethorpes, while the show itself was staged in a field near Grant Thorold Park. Buffalo Bill, who was now in his sixtieth year, gave a demonstration of riding and shooting and the historical recreations included both the attack on the Deadwood stage and the Battle of Little Bighorn – Sitting Bull's son, William, playing the part of his father.

The show continued to tour in Europe and, latterly, North America, until 1913, when it was declared bankrupt. Cody himself had prophesied that it would last until there were no frontiersmen left to travel with it. And so it did. In the latter days, Cody cut costs by taking on local people to help with the day-to-day running of the show. Fred Rye, who became one of the best known showmen in Skegness (see page 71) got his start in the business by working for Cody during the show's Lincolnshire tours.

Most of Cody's Lincolnshire venues have now been built over, but he did leave one lasting legacy, ironically a symbol of the new America. He introduced popcorn to Britain. His audiences munched their way through tons of the stuff, and they've been doing it ever since.

Good Morning Campers!

Billy Butlin is often given the credit for turning Skegness into a thriving seaside resort. However, in 1916, Cox was already describing it as a 'rapidly developing watering place ... crowded

A postcard depicting chalets at Butlin's Skegness in 1939. The sender remarks that the accommodation is 'quite clean and comfortable'. (Author's collection)

and most popular throughout the summer.'

Butlin was a South African by birth. When his parents' marriage broke up, his mother took him to England and then to Canada. After the First World War, he returned to England with just £5 to his name. After spending some years with a travelling fair, he arrived in Skegness where, in 1927, he set up his own permanent fairground. It was very basic to begin with: hoopla stalls, a tower slide, a haunted house experience. Later additions included a zoo and first Dodgem cars to be seen in Britain. It is said that he conceived the idea of a 'holiday camp' while living in Toronto, but it was not until 1936 that he was able to open what was his very first camp.

Actually, it was not the first holiday camp, *per se*. Harry Warner had opened one on Hayling Island in 1932. And it was not sited at Skegness, but at Ingoldmells, over three miles to the north, thus representing competition for the established resort, as opposed to constituting a valuable appendage. Traditional seaside holidays usually involved sojourns in grim boarding houses, run with military precision by sour-faced landladies. Bedrooms were strictly for sleeping only. After breakfast, guests were turned out into the street to 'enjoy' whatever facilities a resort had to offer. In contrast, the Butlin experience offered chalet accommodation, three meals a day and free on-site entertainment – all for £3 a week, Butlin having long-since learned that what he might lose on an individual stay would be more than compensated for by the sheer number of visitors.

The Ingoldmells camp, opened by aviatrix Amy Johnson, was an instant hit. A staff of 'Redcoats' encouraged participation in the entertainment side of the business which, considering the relative isolation of the camp, was essential to its success. The chalets were quite spartan, and remained so for years. One recalls that only cold water was laid on. If you wanted hot water, it was necessary to take a jug and queue up at a dedicated hot water tap. There were communal washing and toilet facilities and a number of dining rooms with timetabled sittings. If you wanted to leave the camp, you were issued with a badge to facilitate re-entry. And, of course, there was the public announcement system, through which the campers were brought to heel every morning and which, on a clear day, could be heard for miles. A major attraction for families was the safe environment the camp provided for children. And Redcoat-run children's activities enabled adults to have time to themselves. Butlin was a familiar figure at the camp, driving around in his Austin 7, with a lion cub as a passenger on the back seat.

Only three years after the camp opened, the Second World War broke out.

During the war years, the Skegness camp was taken over by the navy for use as a training establishment, and was known as *HMS Royal Arthur*. The navy vacated the camp early in 1946 and, despite being the worse for wear, it was refurbished and re-opened to holidaymakers within a few weeks. The late 1940s and the 1950s were golden years for the Butlin empire. Butlin opened the

Ingoldmells Hotel off-site and even built his own airport, where international stars of stage and screen would arrive to perform at the camp.

He was still expanding his business in the 1960s, by which time the continental package tour was starting to impact on the holiday marketplace. The mix of guaranteed sun and exotic locations would soon eclipse the lure of knobbly-knees contests and glamorous granny competitions.

In 1968, for tax reasons, Billy Butlin moved to Jersey, where he remained until his death in 1980. His grave, in the parish of St. John's, is surmounted by a substantial monument in the shape of a king-size bed, sculptured in black marble – a memorial to a showman if ever there was one. Ironically, he never opened one of his own holiday camps in Jersey. This was left to his rival, Fred Pontin.

After his death, attempts were made to show a less genial side to his character. It was said that he used to carry a cut-throat razor in his pocket as protection against the enemies he had made in his journey from poverty to riches. However, a fairground operator's life was not for the faint-hearted. It was – and still is – a tough business. And it is often forgotten that Butlin's name, forever linked with holiday camps, later became synonymous with more than generous financial support for charities.

The Skegness camp still operates, in the guise of 'Funcoast World'. Although one of the original chalets has been preserved for posterity, visitors will wait in vain for the much-loved dawn chorus of *Good Morning Campers!*

Freakshows

In the 1930s, Skegness was flourishing as a seaside resort. It did not possess the brashness of Blackpool or the pedigree of Scarborough, but it suited the holidaymakers from the industrial towns of the East Midlands who flocked there in their thousands, especially during 'factory fortnight' at the end of August when the factories shut down for two weeks.

The visitors were hungry for entertainment and there was plenty on offer. The more outlandish it was, the better they liked it. Amusements included the usual fairground stalls and several features which would be difficult to sustain today, such as two albino girls, remarkable for their white hair and pink eyes and the 'Seal Lion Man', with a deformity of the arms, who would emulate the antics of a sea lion. Billy Butlin, who had his own amusement park, imported a group billed as the 'Royal Midgets' – twelve males and six females, who performed in a revue. He also exhibited 'Princess Ubangi, The Tiny Pigmy Woman', described as 'the cutest little thing ever born'. (Despite, in reality, being neither a pigmy nor a princess, she proved to be a major attraction.)

Another of the resort's showmen was the self-styled 'Captain' Fred Rye, an ex-coal miner who had settled in the area after the First World War. Rye bought Poplar Farm where he bred everything from zebras to snakes. As well as supplying animals to travelling showmen, he ran his own novelty menagerie in a pavilion on Sea View Pullover. Items included 'Beauty and the Beasts', with an attractive blonde reclining on a bed surrounded by animals, and a lion-taming act in which the lions were hypnotised by Ling Foo, a Chinese magician. Rye paid regular visits to Blackpool where, among the infamous freak shows of the Golden Mile, he picked up new ideas and made an occasional purchase. It was here, in 1936, that he acquired two promising exhibits: a cow with five legs and a man called Harold Davidson.

Davidson, an ex-clergyman, was drawing the crowds. For 26 years, he had been Rector of the North Norfolk village of Stiffkey. Instead of confining his activities to his parish, however, he spent most of his time in London, making efforts to save 'fallen' women. Inevitably, he found himself in a number of potentially compromising situations and in 1932 he was defrocked. The loss of his living rendered him destitute. When Rye found him, he was on display in a sideshow, supposedly fasting for a fortnight inside a barrel.

Davidson moved to Skegness for the 1937 summer season. He was not comfortable around animals, but Rye persuaded him to take on the role of lion tamer. At first, all went well, Davidson performing with a single animal. Then he progressed to two: a male, Freddie and a female, Toto. On the evening of 28 July 1937, Davidson was giving his last performance of the day when Freddie attacked him. The cage door was locked and Rye, who had the only key, was at the front of the pavilion manning the ticket booth. Thus, several minutes passed before Davidson could be rescued. Although badly mauled, he was expected to recover, and it came as a shock when he died in Skegness cottage hospital in the early hours of 30 July. Just two days later, Rye was presenting Freddie as 'the actual lion that mauled and caused the death of the ex-Rector of Stiffkey'.

Rye remained in business until the Second World War when visitor numbers declined and it became impossible to get food for the animals, which were gradually sold off. Poplar Farm (on Chapel Lane) now exists in name only, the farm buildings having been developed into holiday cottages and the rest of the land used as a caravan park.

The End of the Pier

The Lincolnshire coast has two recreational piers, one at Cleethorpes and the other at Skegness. Despite several temporary closures in recent years, Cleethorpes pier has proved itself to be one of the most resilient piers in the country. Strongly built in 1873, it withstood a fire in 1903 and survived having a section removed for security purposes during the Second World War.

Skegness pier was a comparatively late starter, opening in 1881. It was 1,817 feet (554 metres) long and, in common with many of its contemporaries, had a 700-seat theatre perched on its seaward end. There was a landing stage, from where a steamship ran day-trips to the Norfolk coast. The history of most piers seems to amount to a catalogue of disasters, and Skegness pier is no exception. The first catastrophe occurred in 1919, when a schooner ploughed into it, splitting it in half. What were intended to be temporary repairs remained in place until 1939, when it was fully restored – only to be partially dismantled almost immediately when war was declared.

After the war, the years of enforced neglect required further renovation.

Surprisingly, the floods of 1953 caused little damage, but the gales of 1978 (which the MET Office famously failed to forecast) destroyed a large section of the pier and left the theatre marooned. In 1985, while the theatre was being demolished, it caught fire and burned down.

The provision of an entertainment facility at the end of the pier was an integral element of a pier's design. In addition to the variety artists who worked within the confines of a grand theatre or concert hall, there were others who performed in the open air at the very end of the pier itself. They were the professional pier divers, men and women who, for the benefit of a paying audience, would dive off the pier into the sea.

Pier divers would often tour the country, making spectacular dives off piers from Blackpool to Bognor Regis. During the summer season, they would make three dives a day, their acts

Skegness Pier in the early twentieth century. (Author's collection)

developing to reflect the increasingly demanding expectations of their audiences. Occasionally, they would dive off the top of buildings sited on the end of the pier, but the entertainment became so popular that scaffolding was erected to increase both the height of the dive and the element of danger. A popular variation on the pier dive, as undertaken by, among others, 'Professor' Bert Powsey, involved riding a bicycle off the pier. Where possible, the run would commence at the landward end, the rider gaining momentum as he sped towards the opposite end, where he would fly through the air before falling to the sea below – the audience wondering how far he would get before gravity forced him down. Although possessing an element of comedy, it could easily turn to tragedy. In 1912, 'Professor Cyril' (Arthur Heppell) lost control of his machine and fatally fractured his skull when he fell.

One of the best-known pier divers was Frank 'Peggy' Gadsby, who sometimes worked for Billy Butlin. Gadsby had the best 'gimmick' of all, for he had only one leg, his right leg having been amputated in childhood. Watching a one-legged man dive from a great height into the sea provided that extra spark of interest for holidaymakers. Gadsby was not the first one-legged pier diver. 'Professor' Billy Thomason – also minus a leg – was doing it as early as 1904, but Gadsby, who was based at Skegness, caught the public imagination in the inter-war years. Sometimes, he would perform at the cricket ground on Richmond Drive, where he dived from a tower into a small tank of water. The tank also contained petrol which would be set alight. Gadsby would then set himself on fire and dive. Powsey performed a similar feat.

Children of pier divers joined their fathers in the business and sometimes performed alongside them. Bert Powsey's daughter, Gladys, performed high diving stunts and almost succeeded in an attempt to swim the English Channel. Similarly, Gadsby's son, Leslie, took up high diving. As the result of an accident sustained in Weston-Super-Mare – he was hit by a rocket fired to signal the start of his performance – his left hand was amputated, but he turned the misfortune to advantage by promoting himself as a one-armed diver. He was also known for his daring rescues of swimmers who got into trouble in the sea off Skegness.

Gadsby Senior's exploits landed him a job as a stunt man in a feature film *Contraband Love* (1931), in which he dived from a cliff at Lizard Point in Cornwall. He was supposed to land in a safety net some 60 feet below, but the net broke and he narrowly avoided ending up on the rocks below. In 1953, the 74-year-old Frank emerged briefly from retirement to stand in for Leslie who was unable to fulfil a high-diving commitment. Frank later admitted to experiencing some qualms at climbing up the ladder but added that he was 'all right coming down'.

Today, most piers are but shadows of their former selves. Skegness pier stretches only to the end of the beach, the modern amusements and facilities being necessarily limited to the shoreward end.

Frank 'Peggy' Gadsby (right), the legendary one-legged pier diver. Apart from regular diving feats from cliffs and piers, Frank also thrilled the crowds with his death-defying dive from a slim scaffolding tower into a small tank of water. This he did at Richmond Drive, Skegness where, for added drama, he would set light to both himself and the surface of the water tank with petrol. The crowds loved it.

'Old Mother Riley'

The critics often panned it, but the kids loved it – the knockabout antics of the Irish washerwoman, Old Mother Riley and
her daughter Kitty. Thanks to Mrs Riley's quick temper, she was
always 'up against it'. Time after time, she would collapse into
a chair, dexterously criss-cross her legs half a dozen times, roll
her eyes and, appealing to Kitty, exclaim in exasperation, 'Oh,
daughter, daughter!'

The act was the creation of comic genius Arthur Lucan, who
was born Arthur Towle in the village of Sibsey, near Boston in
1885. The family later moved to Boston, where Arthur's father
worked as a groom at *The Peacock* in Market Place. As a child,
Arthur did odd jobs in Shodfriars Hall, where theatrical performances often took place. Shortly after the turn of the century, he
left home and began busking in seaside resorts around the country.
Eventually, he joined a pierrot group, 'The Musical Cliftons', with
which he toured. In 1910, the group toured Ireland, where Arthur
eventually struck out on his own as a solo performer, adopting the
stage name of Arthur Lucan – apparently getting the idea from
'Lucan's Dairies', which he saw written on the back of a milk float.

While he was in Dublin, the 28-year-old Arthur met and
married a 16-year-old girl called Kitty McShane. For some years,
the couple performed in pantomime on both sides of the Irish Sea,
Arthur playing the Dame – the basis for the future Old Mother
Riley – for the first time during the First World War. They went
on to develop a music hall act, with Arthur playing an irascible old
woman and Kitty ultimately playing the daughter. In 1923, they
toured South Africa and Australia in the following year.

Back home, they continued starring in reviews and
pantomimes. At this time, their best-known routine was 'The
Match Seller', which would feature in the film, *Old Mother Riley in
Society*. Their most famous sketch, 'Bridget's Night Out', in which
Arthur smashes tons of crockery, premiered just before their Royal

Command Performance, before King George V and Queen Mary, in 1934.

The new routine got its name because Kitty played Bridget, the daughter of Mrs O'Flynn, played by Arthur. It was not until their film career began that Arthur became 'Old Mother Riley' and Kitty became Kitty. The characters were essentially the same but it is surprising what a difference a change of name can make – as Arthur had discovered when he changed Towle to Lucan.

Old Mother Riley was released in 1937. It was so successful that others quickly followed: *Old Mother Riley in Paris* (1938), *Old Mother Riley, MP* (1940), *Old Mother Riley Joins Up* (1940) and *Old Mother Riley in Society* (1940). There was also a series of radio shows for the BBC. They were recorded in front of live audiences and, given that Arthur's comedy was so boisterously visual in nature, one suspects that the listeners at home were often left high and dry. It was at this time that tensions between Arthur and Kitty came to the fore.

Their marriage had always been lively, but life's highway has always been littered with the wreckage of marriages in which husbands and wives have both lived and worked together – and Arthur and Kitty had been touring as a team for 30 years. Eventually, their personal troubles began to overshadow the act, Kitty starting a relationship with an actor called Willer Neal, who often worked with them.

Kitty also earned the reputation of being 'difficult' to work with. Critics complained that she overdressed. However, she was now in her mid-40s and still playing a young girl. What did they expect her to wear? It is also true that she never looks comfortable in front of the cameras, but her role as Arthur's stooge provided few opportunities for development.

The touring and filming continued, but in what would be Arthur's last film, *Mother Riley Meets the Vampire* (1952), he appeared without Kitty, whose on-set altercations with her husband had proved too much for even the most adept of directors to handle. In fact, Arthur and Kitty never performed together again although, despite living openly with Willer Neal, she got into the habit of following Arthur around and giving him a hard time. Arthur also had financial problems. One might have thought that, after a lifetime of gruelling theatrical tours and a successful film career, he would at least have been comfortably off, but this was not the case. Kitty had controlled their finances and, after years of profligate spending, there was nothing left. In 1953, Arthur was declared bankrupt.

At the age of 67, he had to keep on touring in shows, working in order to meet the demands of the Inland Revenue. His style of slapstick comedy was physically demanding, and he had often suffered from ill-health, leading to cancellation of performances here and there. He had an understudy, Roy Rolland, who had performed some stunts for him on screen but, sooner or later, the knockabout stage routines were bound to take their ultimate toll. The end came on the evening of 17th May 1954. The curtain was about to go up at The Tivoli Theatre in Hull for a performance of *Old Mother Riley in Paris* (constructed around the film of the same name) when Arthur, waiting in the wings, dropped dead. Someone was found to take his place and the show went on.

Arthur Lucan was buried in Hull's Eastern Cemetery. Somewhat begrudgingly, Kitty attended his funeral. It probably took her some time to realise that without him, she was nothing. In 1958, she made an unsuccessful attempt to resurrect her career, with Roy Rolland playing Old Mother Riley. She died alone in 1964.

Arthur's grave has become a place of pilgrimage for fans old and new. He has two blue plaques to his name: one adorning the Sibsey cottage where he was born and the other marking his London home in Forty Lane, Wembley. A selection of his films, from a newly (2015) released DVD, are regularly aired on the 'Talking Pictures' TV Channel.

Chapter Eight

COUNTY AT WAR 1914-18

The Grimsby Chums

At the beginning of the First World War, Lord Kitchener, Secretary of State for War, suspected that Britain needed to prepare for a long-drawn-out war of attrition, requiring huge reserves of men. Everyone else envisaged a short, sharp conflict – including the hundreds of thousands of volunteers who flocked to the recruiting stations, fearful that they would miss the chance of a good scrap. By the end of 1914, over a million men had joined up.

Recruitment was helped by the formation of what were known as 'Pals' brigades, established according to the theory that men would be more likely to enlist in the army if they could do so as a group and stick together throughout. So, workers in the City of London formed what became known as the 'Stockbrokers' Battalion'. By and large, however, the pals brigades had their roots in the cities of the north.

One such battalion was raised in Grimsby. At its core were a group of ex-pupils of the Municipal College. They were joined by others from within the town and the outlying villages and called themselves the Grimsby Chums. Officially, at full strength, they were the 10th Battalion of the Lincolnshire Regiment.

Much to their disappointment, the Chums spent the eighteen months following their formation moving around the country from one training camp to another. Even so, however thorough their training may have been, nothing could have prepared them for what they would have to face. They arrived in France on 10th January 1916, finally going into action – and suffering their first casualties – near Armentieres in late February. One of the worst periods they endured covered the opening days of the Battle of the Somme, in July 1916. This was to be the first major test of the volunteer army.

The plan for an all-out assault on the German lines was compromised by a demand from the French to bring it forward, to relieve the pressure on Verdun. Following a massive bombardment of the enemy trenches, the British attacked along a fifteen mile front. The Grimsby Chums were allocated to a section of the line near La Boisselle. On 1st July, they went over the top. Again, plans for a dawn attack were scuppered by the French, and they had to go at 7.30am, in broad daylight. Almost immediately, their slowly advancing ranks were raked with intense machine-gun fire. Those who were able to do so took cover in shell craters – in particular the gigantic 'Lochnagar' crater, a huge depression created by a British mine. After a very few minutes, it was obvious that the plan wasn't working, but further waves of troops were still sent forward. Much of the day was spent in attempts to help the wounded regain the comparative safety of their own trenches. The heady days of recruitment must have seemed far off. The Chums suffered some 500 casualties, including 187 dead. Only now did the disadvantages of forming a 'pals' battalion become apparent. It was said that barely a street in Grimsby was unaffected.

There was a continuous flow of fresh recruits to fill the gaps in the line. So heavy were British losses, however, that, in May 1916, conscription was introduced and, like many of the pals brigades, the Chums lost a little of their cohesion. If anyone let the side down, it was often an outsider. For example, Private Joseph

Chandler of the 10th Lincolnshires, who was executed by a firing squad for a murder committed during a burglary in Calais, came from Gateshead.

Another black day for the Grimsby Chums occurred during the Battle of Arras, which took place from 9th April to 7th May 1917. It followed the pattern of the Battle of the Somme in that French deficiencies led to heavy British casualties. Arras was supposed to divert attention from a major French assault in the south, but the latter failed to get underway on time. The Chums entered the battle towards the end of April, when they moved forward to Roeux. At dawn on 28th April, they advanced on the Germans who were holed up in the village. The houses, left in ruins by the preparatory allied barrage, made excellent machine-gun nests, and the Chums were soon being cut down in a murderous cross-fire. The enemy launched a counter-attack and although the British tried to retreat to their trenches, many were either killed in the attempt or were forced to surrender. Before the morning was over, they had been driven back, but not before the Chums had lost over 400 killed, wounded or missing.

The Grimsby Chums fought on as a unit until the spring of 1918, when

Memorial in Grimsby Minster to the 'Grimsby Chums' who lost their lives in the First World War

the battalion was broken up. It has been suggested that this was primarily because the war was drawing to a close. In fact, some of the bloodiest fighting was to take place during the final months. The simple truth was that after three years of combat, the Pals brigades were exhausted. It was time to hand over the baton, and this became possible with the arrival, in considerable numbers, of Americans. Indeed, while most of the Chums were parcelled off to other units, a limited number were given the job of training these rookies in the exact science of trench warfare.

The 10th Lincolnshires were officially disbanded in June 1919. Although victory parades and celebrations continued for a year after the war had ended, a total of 810 Chums were unable to participate, having made the ultimate sacrifice.

'Little Willie'

Old Lincoln on the hill has its feet in the past; new Lincoln below the hill made the tanks during the war.

(H.V. Morton)

The tank, like the submarine, was first conceptualised centuries before it became a reality. The credit for the invention of the tank is sometimes given to Leonardo da Vinci, who designed a moveable armoured car in the late fifteenth century. It was not until the early twentieth century that the tank became a reality – and it happened in Lincolnshire.

The need for an armoured moving vehicle became apparent during the early stages of the First World War, after artillery barrages had proved ineffective in softening up heavily-defended enemy trenches. Several ideas were bandied about, and serious work began on the development of an armoured vehicle which ran on tracks in February 1915, with the formation of the Landships Committee, an idea of Winston Churchill, who was then First Lord of the Admiralty. The contract for the construction of this revolutionary vehicle was given to William Foster & Company

This unusual memorial to the workers of William Foster & Co. Ltd, who constructed the world's first tanks, stands on the roundabout on Lincoln's Tritton Road – named after the firm's Managing Director, Sir William Tritton

of Lincoln, a manufacturer of agricultural machinery, including threshing machines and tractors. It is said that the word 'tank' was first used by Fosters' workforce owing to the fact that the vehicle resembled a mobile water tank.

What they came up with was 'Number 1 Lincoln Machine', which was about 19 feet in length and nine feet in width, and only just over eight feet high. The design allowed for a two-pounder gun, additional machine guns and a crew of six. It also included two cart wheels appended to the rear to assist steering. This was the protoype of the world's first tank. It was christened 'Little Willie', after Germany's Kaiser Wilhelm II.

A later version, with improvements, was called 'Big Willie'. It was bigger, heavier and carried two six-pounder guns, four machine guns and had a crew of eight. 'Big Willie' was put through its paces in trials carried out in Burton Park, to the north of Lincoln, in January 1916. Apart from an incident in which a shell misfired and was propelled toward Lincoln, the performance satisfied the observers and the model went into production.

What became known as the Mark I tank was used for the first

time in the Battle of Flers-Courcette, fought 15th-22nd September 1916, as part of the Somme offensive. As usual, the objective was to punch a hole in the German front line by throwing a mass of infantry at it. This time, it was hoped that the inclusion of heavy armour would give the assault force the edge. Critics argued that more tests were needed and that the 49 available tanks were insufficient, but General Sir Douglas Haigh, impatient for the ever-elusive breakthrough, insisted on their inclusion in the battle plans.

Notwithstanding the presence of the tanks, the battle followed the pattern of those before and after, with heavy casualties (nearly 30,000) being sustained for an advance which could be measured in yards. The contribution made by the tanks was disappointing. Only 50% got off the mark. Of these, several became bogged down in mud, some lost their tracks and others were hit by artillery shells, which had little difficulty in piercing their light armour. Only a handful reached the enemy lines. The verdict was that they were a useful accessory to the infantry, but nothing more. Churchill and others argued that by his use of the new weapon on such a limited scale, Haigh had thrown away the opportunity for their decisive use at a later stage. However, it was only by testing them in a real battlefield situation that their deficiencies could be identified.

The first battle in which the tank is generally accepted to have made a vital contribution to 'victory' was fought at Cambrai between 20th November and 7th December 1917. Over 300 Mark IV tanks, within a recently-formed dedicated Tank Corps, were amassed for the offensive. The Mark IV was not a great improvement on the Mark I, and tank crews throughout the war had to cope with heat, fumes and deafening noise.

The first day of the battle went well for Haigh, largely because the tanks had managed to forge a path through the enemy's barbed wire defences. It was at a heavy cost, for 180 tanks were either destroyed or suffered mechanical failure. This also meant that the initial success could not be exploited. Over the coming days, the Germans counter-attacked and regained virtually all the territory they had lost. While the massed tank assault at Cambrai may well have been a precursor of things to come, it did nothing to change the all-too-familiar outcome of the battle.

In April 1918, King George V and Queen Mary paid a visit to Lincoln. Their itinerary took in Fosters' factory, where the king asked to take a ride in one of six tanks on display. This was a high point for the firm, which reverted to the production of agricultural products when the war ended. The tanks of the inter-war years were built by Vickers-Armstrong, while the famous Churchill Tank of the Second World War was assembled by Vauxhall Motors. Fosters succumbed to a number of take-overs, finally reaching the end of the line in the late 1960s. The works, in Wellington Street, became a victim of Lincoln's inner-ring road, the site it once proudly occupied now housing a bland retail development. A Mark IV tank is on display in the Museum of Lincolnshire Life, but anyone wishing to see 'Little Willie' must visit the Tank Museum in Bovingdon, Dorset.

The Lincolnshire Zeppelin Raids

During the First World War, German Zeppelins regularly frequented the skies over Lincolnshire. Quite often, they were merely in transit to targets further inland. At other times, Lincolnshire itself was the objective – perhaps Lincoln, one of the industrial hubs of the war effort, or even the Grimsby fishing fleet, at anchor in the North Sea.

From the beginning, the Humber estuary was a valuable point of reference for the Zeppelins and Hull took a continuous battering. The night of 6/7 June 1915 was particularly grim, when Zeppelin L-9 targeted the city centre, leaving a trail of bombed-out buildings and over sixty casualties. Almost as an afterthought, the captain of L-9 bombed Grimsby docks before retiring. He was probably using up what remained of his bomb load, a purpose for which Lincolnshire would prove to be very useful.

Grimsby featured in one of the most controversial episodes of the Zeppelin campaign: the 'King Stephen Incident'. This involved the L-19, which was in action on the night of 31st January/1st February 1916. Following comparatively successful raids on several towns in the west Midlands, L-19 was on the way home when engine trouble led to her ditching in the North Sea, where she was spotted on the morning of 2nd February by a Grimsby trawler, the *King Stephen*. Captain Odo Loewe and his crew – sixteen men in total – were balanced precariously on top of the floating wreckage. The *King Stephen* approached and Lowe asked to be taken aboard. The trawler's skipper, William Martin, refused.

Upon his return to port. Martin reported what had occurred. Royal Navy vessels were sent out in search of the stricken Zeppelin, but it was too late; the L-19 had probably gone to the bottom soon after Martin's departure. In some quarters, Martin was criticised for abandoning the Germans to their fate, although he argued that, had he taken them on board, they could easily have overpowered his crew and taken over the ship. In all probability, this is exactly what would have happened. On the whole, Martin had the support of the nation, for there was little sympathy for the bombing of civilian targets. The German press had a field day, seizing upon the incident for its propaganda value.

Lincolnshire's most devastating raid occurred during the early hours of 1st April 1916. L- 22 dropped several bombs on Humberstone and a few more on Cleethorpes. Little harm was caused at Humberstone, but in Cleethorpes, the Baptist Chapel on Alexandra Road was hit. Normally, the building would have been empty but, as chance would have it, it was being used as accommodation for 70 men of the Manchester Regiment. Thirty-one were killed and many more seriously injured. The latter were taken to a hospital in St. Aidan's Church hall. Many makeshift hospitals had been set up to deal with casualties from the Western Front, but few would have been prepared to cope with such a major incident.

Zeppelin crews found it very difficult to identify their targets.

Blackouts were in force, and any light visible from above, regardless of its location, was often enough to attract a bundle of high explosive or incendiary bombs. Indeed, the residents of isolated Lincolnshire villages sometimes found Zeppelin attacks quite exciting events. On 23rd September 1916, L-14 bombed Washingborough, near Lincoln. The crew may have been targeting the city, an important centre in the production of war materials. The next day, sightseers made their way from Lincoln to view what was actually very limited damage. At the time, a small passenger ferry was used to cross the River Witham and on this day it was so overcrowded that it sank. Two people were drowned.

Like the U-boats, Zeppelins often hunted in packs. Also operating over Lincolnshire on the night of 23/24 September were L-13, L-22, and L-24. The latter, apparently unable to find its primary target, dropped its load on Grimsby on the way home. In fact, the village of Scartho to the south of the town, took

Memorial in Cleethorpes Cemetery to the men of the Manchester Regiment who were killed when a Zeppelin bombed the seaside town's Baptist Chapel

the hit at midnight, although only the Church of St. Giles was damaged. Subsequently, a memorial was erected in the church-yard, commemorating the fact that no one had been hurt. L-22 confined its attentions to the south bank of the Humber, while L-13 bombed the Sleaford area.

The raids, albeit in steadily-declining numbers, continued to the end of the war. One of these was directed specifically at Lincolnshire. On 12/13 April 1918, three Zeppelins – L-60, L-63 and L-64 – ranged widely over the county. Metheringham, where eighteen bombs were dropped, bore the brunt of L-63's effort. L-64 bombed Doddington, Skellingthorpe and Waddington, while L-60 bombed Barton-upon-Humber and Saxby.

The Zeppelin raids of the years 1915-18 had no effect whatsoever on the final outcome of the war, but they did bring a flavour of the horror of warfare to the Home Front. Thanks to advances in the technology of warfare, you could now be blown to pieces hundreds of miles from the battlefield, in the comfort of your own home.

The Airfields

The Royal Flying Corps was formed on 13th May 1912. Originally, it had an army and a navy wing, but the latter was taken out on 1st July 1914, to form the Royal Naval Air Service. On the outbreak of war in August 1914, it was deemed appropriate for the RFC to support army operations in France, while the RNAS took respon-sibility for defending Britain's shores and the skies above them.

As part of its network of defences, the RNAS set up a base at Skegness with a view to patrolling the east coast from the River Humber to The Wash. Skegness was replaced by a base established at Killingholme – nearer to Immingham's precious fuel supplies – and seaplanes, always on the lookout for U-boats, were soon operating from there.

In addition to offshore defence, there was the question of defence against air attacks which although commonplace in the Second World War, were something new in 1915. While the German Zeppelin airships caused little damage, they created a great deal of alarm, and it was necessary to give the impression that something was being done to combat them. The RNAS struggled to tackle the problem and, in 1916, the Royal Flying Corps assumed full responsibility for home air defence.

The RFC had always been based in the south of England, visits to Lincolnshire being limited to refuelling stops on flights to Scotland. Now, a system of Lincolnshire airfields – literally grass fields in the ownership of farmers – had to be set up. Most were situated along the Lincoln Cliff escarpment, from Kirton-in-Lindsey in the north to Leadenham in the south. Beyond the provision of the occasional shed, there was little in the way of facilities.

At first, the only available aircraft were those which had been rejected for service on the Western Front. Even when these were upgraded, it was very difficult to successfully challenge the Zeppelins, which cruised at too great a height. In later years, the German Gotha bombers took over the role of bringing the war to Britain, but – thankfully – they concentrated their efforts on London.

The Lincolnshire airfields were also used in a third role – as training grounds to prepare aircrew for operations overseas. During the First World War, the Germans were always one step ahead in

The Sopwith Camel – the most famous British fighter aircraft of the First World War. Over 1500 were built by the Lincoln firm of Ruston Proctor & Co. Ltd.
(1000aircraftphotos. com)

the development of aircraft. For example, they were the first to perfect a method by which a machine gun could be fired through a moving propeller blade, and the Albatross fighter – as flown by Manfred von Richthoven, the 'Red Baron' – took a heavy toll of British fighters. Thus, the newly-formed training squadrons had their work cut out to keep up with the demand for new pilots.

As always the aircraft were easier to replace than the men. In addition to blazing the trail in the production of tanks, Lincoln was a leading centre of aircraft production. Engineering firms Ruston Proctor & Company, on Waterside, Clayton & Shuttleworth at Stamp End and Robey & Scott on Canwick Road, all of which had specialised in engines and farm machinery before the war, now turned out prodigious quantities of the Sopwith Camel. Clayton & Shuttleworth are credited with building the Camel which shot down von Richthoven.

Sopwith is a name that will always be associated with the British air war. The Sopwith 'Scout', a two-seater introduced in 1914, had the capacity to carry two small bombs under the fuselage. Its weakness was a sudden tendency to go into a spin, earning it the nickname of the 'Spinning Jenny'. The Sopwith 'Pup', a single-seat fighter, introduced into service in 1916 was, as its name suggests, a nippy little machine which played a significant role in the development of early aircraft carriers. The most celebrated model was the 'Camel', also a single-seater fighter, with two synchronised machine guns. First appearing on the western Front in 1917, it was credited with over a thousand enemy 'kills'. The names of these early aircraft suggest something of the cavalier approach to flying in these early days. Some models, such as the 'Bognor Bloater', manufactured by White & Thompson were only ever known by their nicknames.

When the Americans arrived in 1917, they took over RNAS Killingholme – as they would take over many air bases twenty-five years later – and introduced their own Curtiss flying boats. As it happened, the days of the RNAS as a separate entity were numbered for, on 1st April 1918, it was merged with the RFC to form the Royal Air Force.

After the Armistice, the RAF started to decommission the Lincolnshire airfields, until only three were left: Cranwell, Digby and Spitalgate. Of the others, little evidence remains. A grass airstrip still exists at Anwick, near Sleaford, while Leadenham has the remnants of a few brick buildings. Belfast Hangars, which once housed Sopwith Camels, survived at Robey's old test ground at Bracebridge Heath until 2001, when they were unceremoniously demolished. At Killingholme, a portion of the timber slipway lasted until 2007, when it was torn up.

Chapter Nine

ECCLESIASTICAL LINCOLNSHIRE

Gilbert of Sempringham

Gilbert of Sempringham, founder of the Gilbertine monastic order, was born about 1083. His father Jocelin was a wealthy Norman knight who had accompanied William the Conqueror; his mother, a Saxon lady who Jocelin took for his wife.

Initially, Jocelin was greatly disappointed in his son, who suffered from a pronounced physical disability, rendering him unsuitable for the calling of a knight. He was educated in France and, when he returned home, opened a school to provide local children with a basic education. His learning began to win him a reputation, leading to his appointment, in 1122, as a clerk in the household of Robert Bloet, Bishop of Lincoln.

After being ordained by the Bishop, Gilbert was presented to the parishes of Sempringham and West Torrington, where the churches of St. Andrew's and St. Mary's respectively had been expanded by his father. When Jocelin died in 1130, Gilbert began developing a long-standing idea for a religious community. Allegedly unable to find any men willing to commit to the rigours of monastic life, he selected a small number of women, accommodating them in a cloistered enclosure on one of the walls of Sempringham's church. This was the embryo from which the Gilbertine Order evolved.

The first purpose-built Gilbertine monastery began with a grant of land from Gilbert de Gant, who gave three carucates (about 350 acres) for the structure. To begin with, Gilbertine monks followed the rules of St. Augustine while Gilbertine nuns followed those of St. Benedict. As time went on, however, modifications led to the rules acquiring a reputation for being the most austere of any, with scourging liberally prescribed for transgressions. In addition to the standard vows of Chastity, Humility, Charity and Obedience, Gilbertines had to subscribe to a daily diet of a pound of (coarse) bread, two messes of pottage and a draught of water. Clothing and bedding must be 'mean', labour would be great and rest very little.

The Gilbertines received help and encouragement from the government of King Henry II and, in particular, from the Lord Chancellor, Thomas Becket. When the King and Becket fell out over the issue of whether errant clergy should be judged in secular or ecclesiastical courts, Becket fled to France. His friends, the Gilbertines, engineered his escape and then sent him money. Henry could have sent them all into exile, but thought better of it, pledging his continued support for the order.

By 1170, when Gilbert was over 80, there were a dozen Gilbertine Priories – all in Lincolnshire, from Sempringham in the south to Newstead in the north. With the growth of the order came problems. An obvious potential difficulty arose from the Gilbertine model of double-houses, where nuns and monks shared the same site. Safeguards were in place to ensure that they were kept apart. The sisters were penned in by a wall and ditch, 'that no person may go in or have the least sight of them'. If a monk and nun were found guilty of 'sinning carnally together', the man would most be imprisoned and/or expelled, while the woman, 'to avoid the scandal of her wandering abroad', would be placed in solitary confinement, where she would remain 'till death'. Despite these extreme penalties, falls from grace did occur. A sister of Watton Priory became pregnant as a result of a liaison with a lay brother. The girl, after being forced to castrate her lover, was chained up. An investigation censured the nuns and Gilbert himself for negligence. Rumour has it that there were many such departures from chastity.

Lay brothers created many difficulties. Their function was to perform manual labour within the priories and out in the fields. In other orders, there might be as many monks as there were lay brothers, and the work would be distributed among all. In Gilbertine houses, the lay brothers far outnumbered the monks and often resented having to do all the work themselves, especially as they, like the lay sisters, were subject to the same strict rules.

Gilbert died at Sepringham in 1189. He had been blind for several years. In 1202, he was canonised, many miracles of healing having been attributed to him, by 'touching of the clothes ... and also by drinking of the water in which his dead body had been washed'.

The order continued to grow, with houses established in several other counties until, by the mid-fourteenth century, there were a total of 29. The decay of the Gilbertines in the early sixteenth century was probably accelerated by the order's unique dependence upon lay brothers and sisters for, when recruitment declined, they were hit doubly hard. Although the Gilbertines (never a wealthy order) were initially exempted from the Dissolution of the Monasteries, its houses were surrendered voluntarily, Sempringham Priory being signed over to the crown on 18th September 1536. The priory itself was destroyed soon afterwards.

Today, St. Andrew's Church, standing alone in a field above the hamlet of Pointon, is all that remains of Sempringham Priory.

Anne Askew

Anne Askew, one of Lincolnshire's many remarkably strong and single-minded women, was born in 1521, in Stallingborough. Her father, William Askew, was prominent at the court of King Henry VIII. Although William ensured that Anne received a sound basic education, he expected unwavering obedience to his will. He had arranged a marriage between his eldest daughter, Martha, and Thomas Kyme of South Kelsey. When Martha died, he insisted that Anne should take her place as Kyme's wife.

The marriage took place in 1536, when Anne was 15 years old. It proved to be a disastrous union. Two children came of it, but Kyme was a staunch Catholic whereas Anne, through a personal study of the Bible, acquired Protestant beliefs. As a result of ill-treatment at the hands of her husband, Anne was driven from home and travelled to London where, it is said, she sought a divorce – in itself a pioneering aspiration.

Despite failing in her objective, she remained in the capital, where she appears to have consorted with known Protestants and even to have preached in the streets. This led to her arrest, in March 1545. Accused of heresy, she was examined by the Bishop of London, Edmund Bonner. After spending twelve days in prison, she signed a qualified 'confession' and, with the help of family and friends, was bailed on the understanding that she would return home.

Had she remained in Lincolnshire, all would have been well, but the following year, she went back to London and began preaching again. It was bad enough that she had breached the terms of her bail, but during the time she had been away, the political climate had changed. Conservatives within the Church of England encouraged the king to take a far less conciliatory approach with Protestant heretics. In an exercise intended to confirm King Henry VIII's authority as head of the Church of England, Henry agreed to have a number of suspected heretics, including Anne Askew,

The death by burning of Anne Askew, from a woodcut in John Foxe's Book of Martyrs

arrested and held in Newgate prison.

This time, Anne was examined by the Chancellor, Sir Thomas Wriothesley and the Bishop of Winchester, Stephen Gardiner. Over a period of two days, she proved equal to countering the complex theological arguments with which she was confronted. At last, she was taken to the Tower of London where Wriothesley, assisted by Richard Rich, continued the interrogation. Who, they wanted to know, had maintained her while she was in Newgate? She replied that her maid 'went abroad in the streets' and 'made moan to the prentices' who sent her some money. But her inquisitors wanted her to implicate others. When she refused to name names, they ordered her to be racked. The Lieutenant of the Tower, Sir Anthony Knyvett, ordered her to be 'pinched' on the rack and, this being done, was about to release her when Wriothesely demanded that he continue. Kyvett refused and went off to see the king. In his absence, Wriothesley and Rich took over the operation of the rack themselves. Because she 'lay still and did not cry', they continued until 'her bones and joints were almost plucked asunder'.

Finally, they admitted defeat, and Anne was put in a chair and taken to a house where she was put to bed. Again, she was asked to recant and again, she refused. Accordingly, she was returned to Newgate to await execution. While there, she set down a confession of her faith, observing, with regard to the mass, that 'as it is now used in our days, I do say and believe it to be the most abominable idol that is in the world'. She also composed some religious verse, of which the following is a fragment:

> *Yet Lord, I thee desire*
> *For that they do to me*
> *Let them not taste*
> *Of their iniquity*

Anne's end is described by John Foxe in his *Book of Martyrs* (see page 154) On the day of her execution – 16th July 1546 – she was unable to walk and had to be carried to Smithfield. Secured to a stake by means of several chains, she was given a final chance to save herself. Wriothesley assured her that she would receive a pardon from the king if she would only recant, to which she replied that she 'came not hither to deny her Lord and Master'. The faggots were lit and, thanks to a bag of gunpowder which had been tied about her neck, she probably died comparatively quickly. According to eye witnesses, the sky suddenly 'altered colour, and the clouds from above gave a thunder clap', signalling God's anger at 'so tyrannous a murder'.

In her initial attempts to secure a divorce, it is thought that Anne may have consulted the Queen, Henry's sixth and final wife, Catherine Parr. Given Anne's family's connections at court, it is possible that she did gain access to Catherine, whose Protestant sympathies were known to her enemies. It is also likely that Wriothesley had hoped to persuade Anne to identify the queen as one of her confidantes and, although he failed in this objective, Catherine was arrested in the wake of Anne's execution. This time the King, however, was having none of it, and Catherine survived.

John Wesley's Women

John Wesley, the son of Samuel Wesley, Rector of Epworth (see page 203) is renowned as the founder of Methodism. His embarrassingly bizarre relationships with women are often thought to have been inevitable, given his upbringing in a household dominated by them. A year after his birth, which took place in 1703, his elder brother, Samuel Junior, was sent away to school. His younger brother, Charles, was not born until 1707, which meant that he was surrounded by five elder sisters.

Be that as it may, his attitude towards women could well gave been mapped out for him before he breathed his first. His mother, Susanna – herself one of 25 children – gave birth to a total of 19 children. Despite the unequivocal fulfilment of her wifely duties, her husband abandoned her and her offspring in 1701 for a period of one year. The offence she had committed was a refusal to say 'Amen' to his prayer for King William III.

John went up to Oxford in 1720. He was still there in 1724, studying for his M.A. He also fell in love. The object of his attentions was Sarah, sister of a fellow student, Robert Kirkham. Another of Robert's sisters, Damaris, also seems to have expressed an interest in John, but it was Sarah who won his approval. Unfortunately, he could not afford to marry – although one wonders whether improved financial circumstances, would have made any difference to his indecision. At the age of 22, Sarah may have feared being left on the shelf and, finally despairing of John's prevarications, she married John Chapone, a teacher.

The obliging Mr Chapone allowed Sarah to continue seeing John, who was observed holding hands with her while she laid his head on her breast. Meanwhile, during a visit home, he struck up a close friendship with a local girl, Kitty Hargreaves. His father gave her short shrift, but it did him little good, for in 1727, John became curate in the neighbouring parish of Wroot, enabling the couple to see more of each other.

In 1729, John Wesley returned to Oxford to take up the position of lecturer/tutor and formed a new relationship with a 30-year old widow, Mary Pendarves. He also engaged in correspondence with her sister, Anne. This may have been entirely innocent but, as his biographer Stephen Tomkins points out, where John was concerned, spiritual mentoring and romantic passions had a tendency to get 'painfully entangled'.

In 1735, he and Charles left for America, with the aim of preaching and converting the unenlightened folk of Georgia. Here, he became enamoured of Sophy (sic) Hopkey, ward of Tom Causton, a magistrate. Everyone encouraged the budding romance and John went so far as to make a barely disguised proposal of marriage. As was his wont, however, he vacillated, torturing himself with doubts as to whether marriage was consistent with his vocation. While he dithered, Sophy married another – one William Williamson.

John was distraught, particularly as Williamson was not inclined to allow his betrothed the same licence as the charitable Mr Chapone had extended to Sarah. In what was surely a fit of pique, John stopped Sophy from taking Communion and openly condemned what he argued was her lapse into sin. Williamson, acting on behalf of his wife, sued him for defamation of character and had him arrested. John was released without bail, pending his trial. During extended proceedings, however, he absconded, making an unseemly escape under cover of darkness to take a ship back to England.

He arrived in February 1738. Three months later, he underwent his legendary evangelical conversion. Henceforth, he resolved to take his message to the people, preaching throughout the country in the open air, halls, prisons and, eventually, purpose-built Methodist chapels.

Over the next ten years, he had little time for amorous attachments although, among the many thousands who flocked to hear him, there were undoubtedly countless adoring young, unattached women who treasured his every word. Then, in the summer of 1748, he met Grace Murray.

He was staying in Newcastle when he fell ill. Grace, the 32-year-old housekeeper of the local Methodist orphanage, looked after him and was rewarded with one of his ambiguous offers of future married bliss. She subsequently accompanied him on his peregrinations and was still in tow a year later, during an extended preaching tour of Ireland. Like Sophy, however, Grace had a reserve suitor waiting in the wings – another Methodist preacher called Bennett, whose matrimonial ambitions were openly encouraged by Charles Wesley, who did not approve of Grace as a wife for his brother. When Grace and Bennett finally tied the knot, John's reaction was characteristically splenetic.

A year later, John met a 41-year-old widow, Mary Vazeille. She differed from his previous love interests in that her late husband had left her well provided for, She also had several children. Even though she must have been aware of his chequered past when it came to affairs of the heart, she accepted his proposal of marriage. Miraculously, he kept to it and, despite the customary opposition from Charles Wesley, the wedding took place in 1751. Almost inevitably the union quickly descended into a tragic comedy. John expected Mary to withstand the same hardships as he cheerfully accepted. The family was dragged around on the demanding preaching circuit, the rigours of which often involved enduring physical assault by unenlightened mobs.

In theory, the marriage lasted 20 years, for Mary did not finally leave him until the early 1770s. In practice, it had been a marriage in name only long before the final parting. Mary was particularly perturbed by his correspondence with other women, and she did not take it lying down. She was once observed frenziedly dragging John around the room by his hair. When Mary died, he did not even attend her funeral.

John Wesley died in 1791. The nature of his personal relationships defies explanation. He was no misogynist, for he promoted the liberation of women, even going so far as to encourage them to take up preaching. Perhaps the real problem lay with marriage as an institution, for how could either a man or a woman fulfil their marriage vows when it was the duty of both to devote their lives wholly to God's work?

The Gypsy's Parson

I can generally tell any gypsy whom I meet who his grandfather was. (George Hall)

Lincolnshire villages, regardless of their size, always have a church. Sometimes, a substantial place of worship is surrounded by a mere handful of cottages, and one might wonder how a rector with such a small flock of souls to save would occupy his time. The answer is that a great many of them had other interests which their ecclesiastical 'living' (a house and income) allowed them to pursue. For example, Charles Hudson, Rector of St. James's, Skillington, indulged in mountaineering – meeting his death in 1865, while scaling the Matterhorn. Thomas Townsend, Vicar of St. Nicholas's, Searby, was notable for his woodcarving skills, expressed throughout

his church. Another clergyman with a hobby which monopolised a good deal of his time was George Hall, Vicar of St. Olave's, Ruckland – a hamlet with a population of 24. Hall's speciality was the Romany gypsy.

George Hall was born and raised in Lincoln. In a narrow court between his father's house, off Bailgate, and West Common, a gypsy community had

The Reverend George Hall, 'The Gypsy's Parson'

established itself. Hall came into contact with some of the children during his early schooldays in the neighbourhood. The spell they cast upon him was later reinforced by his reading of George Borrow's autobiographical novels, *Lavengro* and *The Romany Rye*. Thereafter, every spare moment was spent in learning, at first hand, as much as he could about their way of life – so much so that he became known as 'The Gypsy's Parson'. In 1916, he published a memoir of his experiences under this title.

Hall made a point of visiting horse fairs, for he knew that gypsies were always to be found there. Horncastle Horse Fair grew to become the largest in Europe and, Hall notes, 'members of our best gypsy families invariably made a point of attending'. The 'better sort' of gypsies would camp in a field to the rear of St. Mary's Church, while the poorer families camped in Hemingby Lane or in the yard of the *New Inn*. They were not above engaging in sharp practice for, as one remarked, lying for a living was essential, 'else how could any sort of business be carried on?'

Nonetheless, Hall thought that the law victimised gypsies, referring to 'the unedifying spectacle of British justices vying with one another in their ardour for dispatching gypsies across the sea on the most trivial pretexts'. All the elderly gypsies with whom Hall met had what they called 'transportation tales' to relate. There was the tale of a Romany mother, sent to Van Diemen's Land [Tasmania] 'for stealing a lady's comb valued at sixpence' and another of a middle-aged gypsy transported for seven years for the crime of 'appropriating three penny-picture books from a cottage doorway'.

Gypsies were sometimes apprehended for the theft of livestock – particularly sheep – for which the standard sentence was death, usually commuted to a lengthy term of transportation. Perhaps Hall is a little partisan in his suggestion that gypsies were unfairly singled out. The law was harsh but, in Lincolnshire at least, it appears to have been applied consistently to gypsies and non-gypsies alike.

It was not unusual for Hall to be invited to join a band of gypsies for a meal. In this connection, he observes that they were always fond of roast hedgehog which, 'accompanied with sage and onions is a dish for an Episcopal table', with its pleasing blend of 'pheasant and sucking-pig'. Acceptance into Romany circles was never a problem for him because, having taken the trouble to learn the gypsy dialect, he could converse with them on their own terms. He did encounter some resistance when he tried to take photographs. One girl initially refused because she thought it would bring her bad luck, but relented when he gave her a pair of bootlaces. Others would not agree to be 'took' at any price, for they were a notoriously superstitious people, particularly when it came to births and deaths.

When a child was born, breadcrumbs would be strewn around the tent to ward off any evil influences. In addition, it was customary for a plate, cup and saucer to be set aside for a mother's use for a period of four weeks following the birth of a child. Upon the expiry of this period, they were destroyed. When a gypsy died, no one would utter his or her name. If they were to do so, it would raise the ghost of the deceased. One man whose son had died even invented a nickname for a friend who bore the same name in order to avoid pronouncing the name of the dead child. And there was a strong belief in omens of death. A man whose wife had been taken into hospital knew that she had died because 'two crows and two yellow pigeons flew to and fro' over him in the early morning.

For all that, gypsy women were always happy to engage in the business of fortune-telling. Hall spoke with a woman who had set up a tent at Cleethorpes. She laughed at the foolishness of the young women who came to see her, gazing into her crystal ball in the expectation of seeing the faces of their future husbands. Another asked Hall to explain the difference between a gypsy telling fortunes at a fair and a parson preaching in church. She described herself as a low-class fortune teller and Hall as a high-class fortune teller. After all, she added, 'when folks do bad things, you foretell a bad future for them ... and when they do right, you promises 'em a good time.' The only difference between them, she insisted, was that Hall had the advantage of a good education.

It was fortunate that Hall did, indeed, have a good education, for otherwise, much of the folklore relating to gypsy life would have been lost for ever. He was a stalwart member of the Gypsy Lore Society in its fledgling years, his papers forming a valuable part of its collection.

The Wakeford Case

On 4th February 1921, John Wakeford, the 60-year-old Precentor of Lincoln Cathedral and Archdeacon of Stow, appeared before an ecclesiastical court to face charges relating to the Clergy Discipline Act of 1892. It was alleged that on two occasions, in March and April 1920, Wakeford had stayed at the Bull Hotel in Peterborough with a woman who was not his wife.

According to the prosecution, on the evening of 14th March, Wakeford and a young woman had arrived at the Bull, where they shared a double-bedded room for two nights. The proprietor of the Bull and hotel staff attested to this, pointing out that the girl wore no wedding ring. Moreover, on the morning of 15th March, the Dean of Peterborough Cathedral had seen Wakeford (whom he recognised) and a woman walking around the building. The couple stayed at the Bull Hotel for a second time on the evening of 2ndApril. On this occasion, their presence was confirmed by the police, who were there on another matter.

In his defence, Wakeford said that he had gone to Peterborough in March so that he could be alone to prepare a series of sermons he was due to deliver. He arrived at the Bull Hotel alone and he stayed there alone. He spent the morning of 15th March in Peterborough Cathedral, working on his sermons. While there, he met a girl who was looking around, and this must have been the person noticed by the Dean. He spoke with her and the pair walked to a local shop, where Wakeford told her she could buy a picture postcard of a memorial she had been viewing. He had visited the hotel in April, he claimed, only to break his train journey between London (where he had been preaching) and Lincoln.

The evidence against him appeared to be overwhelming, and he was found guilty. He had a right of appeal, and it was at the appeal hearing that Wakeford argued he was the victim, of a conspiracy.

John Wakeford was a man who made enemies very easily. Lacking the advantages possessed by most of the senior clergy of Lincoln Cathedral, he had struggled to succeed, and never really fitted in. One of his enemies was his wife's elder brother, Herbert Worthington, Rector of Cadeby in Leicestershire. Worthington felt that his sister – Evelyn – had married beneath her. Over the years, he came to believe that her husband had brought her great unhappiness, and he played a prominent role in bringing the charges against him.

Wakeford was more proactive in incurring the wrath of a second individual. In his capacity of Archdeacon, Wakeford was responsible for twenty-one Lincolnshire deaneries. Included within the deanery of Horncastle was the parish of Kirkstead and, adjoining the ruins of Kirkstead Abbey, the disused Church of St. Leonard. The land upon which it stood was owned by the Reverend Charles Moore, Rector of Appleby Magna, near Peterborough. Shocked at the poor state of repair of the church, Wakeford caused a lot of trouble for Moore, arranged for the renovation of the church and, in addition to his other duties, took on the living on Kirskstead. Moore was incensed – not least because he had to pay Wakeford's stipend. He also believed that Wakeford was behind a charge of immorality that was levelled against him.

Moore and Herbert Worthington were close friends, and it was Wakeford's contention that the two men, scheming to bring about his downfall, had used his visits to the Bull Hotel to set him up. It seemed unlikely, given the number of people who would have had to be brought into the plot, and Wakeford's appeal against the original decision failed.

By this time, the 'Wakeford Case' was attracting considerable public attention. Opinion was firmly divided, between those who were in no doubt as to Wakeford's guilt and those who were convinced of his innocence. There was no middle ground.

This schism was mirrored in press reports of the verdict. *The Times* expressed its disbelief that Wakeford, in broad daylight and clad in his clerical garb, would have taken a woman to a busy hotel for immoral purposes. *The Daily Express*, on the other hand, felt that 'justice had been applied'. *The Spectator* agreed, making the fair point that it would have been difficult for Wakeford to have

St. Leonard's Church, Kirkstead, which came under the critical eye of Archdeacon Wakeford

been the victim of a pre-arranged conspiracy simply because he had made no prior plans to stay at the Bull Hotel.

One publication, however, went to extremes in its support of the disgraced clergyman, taking up his cause with a vengeance: the weekly publication *John Bull*. Its disreputable owner, Horatio Bottomley, probably gave little thought to Wakeford's guilt or innocence. He merely saw the affair as a budding *cause celebre* that had the potential to revive the paper's flagging circulation figures. *John Bull's* crusade revolved around finding the girl in the Cathedral – 'the Wakeford Woman' – and offering her £2,000 to make herself known. A woman called Freda Hansen did come forward to claim the money, and even though she signed a declaration that she was, indeed, the girl who had spoken with Wakeford, it did not materially affect the prosecution's case that he had been accompanied by a woman at the hotel.

Bottomley then sent Wakeford – now deprived of his livelihood – on an inspired whistle-stop tour of the country. In innumerable cinemas and hired halls, Wakeford would state his case as a prelude to a short dramatic motion picture, entitled 'The Mystery of the Wakeford Case'. When, a year later, the public tired of the cause, *John Bull* dropped it. In truth, nothing else could be done. At the invitation of a fellow clergyman, Wakeford and his wife moved to a small bungalow in Biggin Hill, Kent, where they eked out a living from keeping poultry.

John Wakeford died in 1930, after spending two years in the Kent County Lunatic Asylum, to which he had been committed when, inevitably, his mind was finally overwhelmed by the burden of his misfortunes.

Chapter Ten

PIONEERS

John Smith & Pocahontas

John Smith, the son of a farmer, was born in 1580, in Willoughby, near Alford. He attended school in Louth and, at the age of 16, embarked on a career as a soldier of fortune. For the next eight years, he served in a number of continental armies, earning promotion to the rank of captain. He endured many hardships, including an episode when he was captured by the Turks and sold into slavery.

Returning to England, he became interested in the plans of the newly established Virginia Company of London to establish a base in North America with a view to exploiting the deposits of gold and silver with which the new continent was surely richly endowed. As an experienced soldier, Smith would have been reckoned a valuable addition to the first group of colonists getting ready to embark.

There were over one hundred of them, setting sail in December 1606 in three ships. During the passage, Smith became obstreperous and was locked up. When, after an arduous voyage, the vessels made landfall, in April 1607, sealed Virginia Company orders were opened and, to everyone's surprise, Smith had been named as one of the members of the ruling council.

The site was selected for what would become Jamestown and building began. From the start, the colonists' main problem was the lack of food. There was little left over from the voyage, and the Native Americans, with whom the colonists soon came into contact, were wary of the strange intruders. However, it was hoped that the little food which the natives were prepared to barter, coupled with a reasonable supply of deer and wildfowl, would enable Jamestown to survive until fresh supply ships arrived.

In December 1607, Smith led a small party to explore the upper reaches of the Chickahominy River. While thus engaged, he was captured by Opechancanough, a brother of Powhatan, chief of the Powhatan confederacy of Native American tribes. For a few excruciating moments, it seemed to Smith that he was about to die, but he succeeded in arousing Opechancanough's curiosity by producing his compass. It was just possible that Smith was a leader, a man of significance. If so, then it would be advisable to bring him before Powhatan.

This did not happen straight away. Perhaps anxious to bask in the glory of his important (or so he hoped) catch, Opechancanough spent several days parading Smith through native villages. Smith was treated well and dined sumptuously. How was it possible, he wondered, for these people to live so well when the colonists were permanently on the verge of starvation?

Finally, on 30th December, Smith was brought to Powhatan's capital, Werowocomoco, where he was brought before the great chief himself. Questioned about the aims of the settlers, Smith tried to convince Powhatan that their stay would be only temporary. His story did not go down too well and he was led to a place of execution and his head forced down onto a stone. As clubs were raised to beat his brains out, one of the most famous scenes in history was enacted: Powhatan's favourite daughter, Pocahontas, ran forward and, shielding Smith's body with her own, pleaded for his life. Powhatan was won over. Two days later, in return for an undertaking to supply the natives with guns and a grindstone, Smith was escorted back to Jamestown.

Any attempt to analyse the motives of Pocahontas in saving Smith from a grisly fate must take account of the fact that she was about 12 years of age at the time. Smith thought she was only ten. It is possible that she was hoping to receive exciting new gifts from the colonists. She was certainly intrigued by them and years later, when push came to shove, she chose to live among them. Whatever goodwill, if any, Powhatan himself may have had towards the settlers evaporated when more boatloads began to arrive.

In September 1608, against all the odds, Smith was chosen to be president of the governing council, and lost no time in acquiring a reputation as a martinet. Arguably, this is what the colony needed to stop it from falling apart, but his authoritarianism earned him many enemies.

Towards the end of the year, at Powhatan's invitation, Smith led an embassy to Werowocomoco with a view to bargaining for food. Again, Powhatan primarily wanted guns, but Smith hoped to talk him out of it. The talks did not go well, and on the evening of his second day in the village, Smith was approached by Pocahontas, who warned him that her father had plans to kill him that very night. The Englishmen set a vigilant watch and, as a result, the attack failed to materialise. Once again, Pocahontas had saved Smith's life.

Romance may have been in the air, but it was not fated to materialise. A few months later, during an exercise to disperse some of the settlers by establishing a new community, Smith was seriously injured in an explosion. He had settled down to rest when a spark – possibly from someone's pipe – ignited the powder bag hanging from his belt. Badly burned and in great pain, he was carried back to Jamestown where, he later maintained, a plot to kill him was hatched.

His term of office as president of Jamestown was coming to an end, and he suspected that his enemies would take advantage of the opportunity to destroy him. Accordingly, he arranged passage for himself on the next available ship leaving for England. The settlers told Pocahontas that he had died. The fact that she did not visit Jamestown for several years afterwards is an indication of the genuine affection she felt for him.

John Smith and Pocahontas would meet for one last time seven years later. Another colonist, John Rolfe fell in love with her and, in April 1614, the couple were married at Jamestown. Rolfe brought his new bride to London. She arrived to discover for the first time that Smith was still very much alive. Their meeting, though inevitable, was awkward and strained. Smith had known it would be so. They exchanged pleasantries and engaged in polite conversation concerning their respective experiences since their last encounter. Smith was keen to return to the New World, but Pocahontas hoped to make London her home.

Neither left England again. Pocahontas succumbed to the foul air of the capital and died in March 1617, while Smith survived until 1631. He never married.

The Man Who Ate His Boots

Sir John Franklin is the most famous son of Spilsby, the market town where he was born in 1786. From an early age, he hankered after going to sea. His initial experiences in the Royal Navy included participation in the Battle of Trafalgar in 1805 and involvement in an expedition to Australia led by his cousin, Matthew Flinders.

The venture with which Franklin's name came to be inextricably linked, however, was the search for the North-west Passage – a sea route linking the Atlantic and Pacific Oceans, which would provide a direct trade route to the countries of the Orient. In 1819, the Royal Navy planned a two-pronged assault on the problem. Lieutenant William Parry would seek an entrance to the Passage via Lancaster Sound, while a second party, which Lieutenant John Franklin was selected to lead, would travel overland to map part of the North Canadian coastline.

The expedition was poorly financed – Franklin's party numbered only five men, including himself – and would be dependent for its success upon the co-operation of the big trading companies and local communities of trappers and Native Americans. Having sailed from Gravesend on 23rd May 1819, Franklin arrived at York Factory, on the western shores of Hudson Bay on 30th August. A cursory glance at a relief map of Canada illustrates the colossal task Franklin had ahead of him.

The small group set out from York Factory on 19th September, making its way overland to the Saskatchewan River and then, in stages, to Great Slave Lake. The outposts they visited were unable to spare them supplies, compelling them to hunt for food en route, thus limiting their progress. Had they not acquired the services of several trappers and Native Americans, they would have starved. On 20th August 1820, they reached Winter Lake, where they settled in for the winter. On 14th June 1821, they set off north and followed the Coppermine River to the Arctic Ocean, which they reached on 21st August 1821.

Having achieved his goal, Franklin found himself facing the same problem as Captain Scott would experience on reaching the South Pole in 1912: he had to summon up the energy and resources to do the return trip. Undaunted, he explored part of the coastline before deciding to follow the River Hood (which flowed into Bathurst Inlet) and then strike across country to pick up the Coppermine River, from where he would make his way back to Winter Lake. The hunting was poor and the group was soon in dire straits. Franklin and four others pressed ahead to their old winter quarters on Winter Lake, arriving on 11th October 1821. They had expected to find food which the Yellowknife tribe had agreed to supply in readiness for their return, but nothing was there.

For the next few weeks, the party survived by eating scraps of lichen and strips of leather cut from old shoes. Finally, on 7th November, one of Franklin's companions who had been left behind arrived with a party of natives who he had stumbled upon.

It would still be a difficult, tedious journey back to York Factory, but the survivors, who had long since been given up for dead, arrived in July 1822, after a journey of more than 5,000 miles.

Franklin's experiences earned him the soubriquet 'The Man Who Ate His Boots'. There were even some who suggested that members of the expedition had been reduced to eating their dead comrades. However, when he returned home, he was promoted to captain and lionized by society. In 1825-27, he undertook a second expedition to Canada, focussing on an exploration of the MacKenzie River. It was well planned and more measured in terms of its objectives, and this time his boots remained intact.

In 1836, Franklin (by now, Sir John) was appointed Lieutenant-Governor of Van Diemen's Land. He and his wife achieved much in terms of developing this minor penal colony but, as a naval officer, Franklin was used to toeing the line, and expected others to do the same. When he was recalled, in 1843, it was in less than happy circumstances.

At this point, retirement should have beckoned, but Franklin was determined to remain in harness. When, two years later, James Clark Ross turned down the opportunity of leading yet another expedition in search of the North-west Passage, the 59-year-old Franklin jumped at the chance to take on the job.

This expedition, well planned and provisioned for a three-year voyage, comprised two ships, HMS *Erebus* and HMS *Terror*, with a complement of 24 officers and 110 men. Like all Arctic explorers, Franklin possessed more than his fair share of optimism, but his confidence was shaken by a curious incident that occurred during the preparations for his departure. His wife had just finished making a Union Jack flag which he was to take with him. As he lay on a sofa, she threw it over him, an innocent action which, nevertheless, he interpreted as an ill omen, owing to the fact that the Union Jack was used as a shroud for those buried at sea.

On 19th May 1845, the expedition set sail from Greenhithe. It was last seen two months later by the crew of a whaler,

Statue of Sir John Franklin in his home town of Spilsby

who came across the two ships in Lancaster Sound. One hundred and seventy years on, the fate of Franklin and his fellow explorers is still being pieced together.

Under pressure from Lady Franklin, the Admiralty mounted its first 'rescue' mission in 1848, but it was not until 1850 that something was found: three graves amid the remains of a camp on Beechey Island. Over the next few years, the Inuit people reported having encountered parties of Europeans who had starved to death, and produced items of cutlery in support of their claims. It was also suggested that, in their extremity, the doomed men had resorted to cannibalism.

All members of the Franklin Expedition were declared dead as of 31st March 1854, but in 1857, Lady Franklin financed her own expedition, which discovered a cairn containing messages on King William Island. One of these messages, dated 25th April 1848, told the story of Franklin's fate. The ships had been trapped in the ice for eighteen months, during which time Franklin and twenty-four others had died. The 105 survivors were going to attempt the well-nigh impossible task of walking to safety. The most poignant discovery was a lifeboat containing an accumulation of items, including books, superfluous to the survival of the dying individuals who planned to drag it across the frozen wastes.

A contributory cause of Franklin's own death and the deaths of many of his crew may have been lead poisoning owing, in part, to the nature of contemporary food canning processes. This was confirmed in the 1980s, by an examination of the three bodies discovered at Beechey Island. Most recently (2014), the wreck of HMS *Erebus* was discovered on the sea bed in Queen Maud Gulf, off the North Canadian mainland, suggesting, intriguingly, that some of the crew may have returned to the vessel. HMS *Erebus* was Franklin's own ship and Queen Maud Gulf is a comparatively short distance from Bathurst Inlet, scene of his earlier exploits. Thus, in spirit at least, Sir John had come full circle.

Into Thin Air

Advances in aircraft design that took place during the First World War gave a tremendous fillip to the expansion of commercial air travel. In Germany, DELAG had been running commercial airship flights since 1909, but the first fixed-wing commercial ventures did not appear until the immediate post-war years. Even then, the first airlines had to build their services around the provision of facilities for the fortunate few.

One of the earliest civil airline pilots was Captain Walter Raymond Hinchliffe (who chose to call himself by his second forename). Like many of his colleagues, Hinchliffe had been a First World War fighter ace and was credited with six 'kills' between February and May, 1918. During the course of his wartime exploits, he had lost his left eye, and wore an eye-patch to conceal the disfigurement. The wound may have been sustained when his Sopwith Camel burst a tyre on landing, although Hinchliffe himself claimed to have sustained the wound during an encounter with German Gotha bombers. According to other accounts, he had come off worst in a tussle with von Richthoven, the 'Red Baron'.

However the injury happened, one would have thought that his flying days were over. Such was his skill in the air, however, that after the war, civil airlines had no qualms about employing him. He worked for the Dutch airline, KLM, founded in 1919, and then for the British airline, Instone Airlines, which was later absorbed into British Imperial Airways, for whom he was still working in 1928. The strain placed upon his one good eye was beginning to tell, and he had begun to worry what the future might hold for him when there arose an opportunity which, if it could only be grasped, promised to set him up for life: he was introduced to a glamorous socialite, Elsie MacKay.

·   Elsie was the daughter of Lord Inchcape, the P&O shipping magnate. Multi-talented and self-assured, she was something of a tearaway. In 1917, she had eloped with an actor, Dennis Wyndham – who later became well-known playing the villain in Will Hay films of the 1930s. As 'Poppy' Wyndham, Elsie herself appeared in several films of the silent era. Whatever she wanted, she always got, by hook or by crook. She was a keen flyer and had conceived the notion of becoming the first woman to fly across the Atlantic.

Exploration of the air was all the rage, if only because there was nothing left on terra firma to discover. The last great wildernesses, the Polar icecaps, had been conquered before the war, Peary having reached the North Pole in 1909 and Amundsen the South Pole two years later.

Aviation also held the attraction of being a sphere in which women could make their mark, especially if they were well-to-do – like Mary Russell, Duchess of Bedford, who made two record breaking flights, or Mildred, the Honourable Mrs Victor Bruce who, taking a passing fancy to a Blackburn Bluebird she saw in a showroom one day, decided to fly around the world in it.

When someone told Elsie that Raymond Hinchliffe was possibly the most outstanding pilot of his day, she decided that he must be the one to help her bring this, her latest dream, to fruition. It was rumoured that, as a result of her marriage to Wyndham, Elsie had been disinherited, but she was still comfortably off. Over lunch at the Ritz, she made Hinchliffe a very generous offer: £80 per month plus expenses, his own choice of aeroplane and any prize money for accompanying her across the Atlantic. She even threw in a £10,000 life insurance policy as protection for his wife, Emily and their two daughters. Hinchliffe thought the matter over carefully. Only the previous year, he had been involved in unsuccessful negotiations of a similar nature with another heiress, Mabel Boll. Unlike Ms Boll, however, Elsie was an accomplished pilot in her own right and this decided Hinchliffe in her favour. She sent him over to America to buy a suitable aircraft. He selected the Stinson Detroiter – a single-engine (220hp) six-seat monoplane with all the latest gadgets, including an electric starter and a heated cabin. Hinchliffe did not only know how to fly a plane: he also knew how to choose one.

A difficult and unusual problem regarding arrangements for the venture was the necessity for secrecy. Elsie was 34 years old, but had her father known of her intentions, he would have done everything in his not inconsiderable power to prevent her carrying them out. So, pains were taken to ensure that she appeared only as financier, with a friend of Hinchliffe's, Gordon Sinclair, being presented to the world as co-pilot.

Elsie demonstrated her personal clout by persuading the RAF to let her use RAF Cranwell for the flight – an essential prerequisite as Cranwell possessed the only runway in the country that was long enough to give the heavy Detroiter (named 'Endeavour') any chance at all of getting airborne.

In fact, throughout the late 1920s and the 1930s, Cranwell was used in several world record challenges. In 1927, three attempts were made on the long-distance flying record. The first one succeeded, but the new record of 3,419 miles (from Cranwell to the Persian Gulf) was itself broken within a few hours by Charles Lindberg's New York to Paris flight.

The early days of March 1928 saw Hinchliffe and his wife, together with Gordon Sinclair and Elsie ensconced at *The George* in Leadenham, making plans for the departure. Although money was no object, the team's preparations were quite hurried. The RAF wanted them out of the way as quickly as possible. Lord Inchcape was also sniffing around and Elsie despaired of her ability to keep up the pretence for much longer. There was also the worrying prospect that they might be pipped at the post by a rival German team that had set up camp in Ireland. On top of everything, Hinchliffe had lost his job, Imperials Airways having refused to grant him leave of absence. Against his better judgement, therefore, Hinchliffe agreed to start on 13th March.

The weather forecast that day was atrocious, but 'Endeavour' took off at 0835 hours amid snowdrifts and a bitterly cold westerly wind. At the very last moment, Hinchliffe tried to dissuade Elsie from accompanying him, but Elsie would not be discouraged. And so, 'Endeavour' struggled into the air. As she did so, there was some suggestion that the wind seemed to be shifting around to the east, in her favour, but when last seen, off the Irish coast at around 1330 hours, she still seemed to be struggling against a head wind. Further out in the Atlantic, storm clouds were gathering.

The month of March is traditionally the worst month of the year for air disasters. More fatal crashes occur in this month than in any other. In many cases, severe air turbulence is the cause. The 'Endeavour', buffeted about amid North Atlantic gales, with a weary Hinchliffe at the controls, is not a pleasant picture on which to dwell. The aircraft had no radio – one was available, but Elsie decreed that it would constitute excess weight – while such preliminary trials as 'Endeavour' had undergone revealed both compass and fuel supply problems which Hinchliffe doubtless would have preferred to see rectified. And, like all wartime pilots, he was superstitious and felt uncomfortable about flying on the thirteenth day of the month. Even so, the last entry in the diary which he had left with Sinclair read: 'My confidence in the success of the venture is now 100%.'

All other factors being equal, 'Endeavour' should have reached its destination – Newfoundland – in twenty-eight hours. She had sufficient fuel for up to forty hours and so, even with a head wind, there should not have been a problem. That there *was* a problem became apparent as soon as the Stinson's maximum flying time elapsed, with daily newspapers of 15th March carrying headlines such as 'Fuel limit long passed'. There were numerous false sightings in the skies over Philadelphia and faint hopes that the plane had landed in an inhospitable part of Newfoundland. But it was no good. Raymond Hinchliffe and Elsie MacKay were never seen again.

Left in dire financial straits, Emily Hinchliffe applied to Lord Inchcape for the balance of her husband's salary, but the millionaire responded by freezing all Elsie's assets – eventually bequeathing the realized total sum to the government in order to help pay off the national debt. Even the insurance company initially refused to pay out on the £10,000 insurance policy, on the grounds that the premiums had not been properly paid. This should have been the bitter end of the story, but the strangest part of all was yet to come.

On 13th April, Mrs Hinchliffe received a letter from a Mrs Beatrice Earl of Surrey. Mrs Earl dabbled in spiritualism and the occult in an effort to 'make contact' with her son who had been killed during the war. At the end of March, with this aim in mind, she had been working in the comfort of her own home with a Ouija board. Instead of providing her with a consoling message from her son beyond the grave, the instrument spelt out a very different message:

I was drowned with Elsie MacKay ... Fog, storm winds, went down from great height ... Off Leeward Islands. Tell my wife I want to speak to her. Am in great distress.

Mrs Earl also wrote to Sir Arthur Conan Doyle, who arranged for her to have a sitting with Eileen Garrett. One of the most respected mediums of her generation, Mrs Garrett spent as much time being tested by various psychical research groups as she did passing on messages to the bereaved from the spirit world. During the sitting, Mrs Garrett's spirit guide, Ulvani, reiterated the information that Hinchliffe was desperate to speak with his wife. Emily had little truck with spiritualism, but when Conan Doyle wrote to her personally, she agreed to meet Mrs Garrett.

On 22nd May 1928, Emily had her first sitting with Mrs Garrett. Many meetings between the two women followed as the once sceptical Emily grew into a convinced believer. Through Ulvani (and occasionally in his own voice) Hinchliffe provided details of his personal possessions, deceased friends and other stock-in-trade elements of the professional medium's repertoire. Regarding the circumstances of his death, he spoke of encountering very strong winds that broke the aeroplane's wing strut, forcing him to veer to the south. Making for the Azores with a faulty compass and oiled-up spark plugs, he was forced to ditch a mile offshore. He drowned twenty minutes after leaving the wreck. Elsie drowned inside the cabin.

This information conflicted in part with the information provided by Mrs Earl's Ouija board with regard to the Leeward Islands. Conan Doyle, anxious not to allow such details to obscure the bigger picture, suggested that this reference was a misinterpretation of 'to the leeward of the Azores'. In December 1928, the wheels belonging to 'Endeavour' were washed up on the coast of County Donegal, suggesting that the tragedy had occurred sooner, rather than later in the flight.

Even now, the story was not quite finished, for Hinchliffe subsequently predicted the R101 Airship disaster. In terms of long distance air travel, airships were still thought to have a great future. The R101, a hydrogen-filled monster, 731 feet (223 metres) in length, was the largest airship in the world, and something of which the British government was immensely proud.

In September 1929, during one of Emily Hinchliffe's sittings with Mrs Garrett, her husband's spirit came through with a warning for his friend, Ernest Johnson, navigator of the R101, not to fly on it. A little over a year later, on its maiden voyage, the R101 crashed at Beauvais in France, killing 48 of the 54 people on board – including Johnson. It would appear that old airmen, like old soldiers, never die.

Chapter Eleven

BOMBER COUNTY 1939-45

The Dambusters and Lincolnshire's Air War

Airfields have flayed it bare.....
(W.G. Hoskins)

The end of the First World War was only the beginning for the fledgling Royal Air Force – and Lincolnshire would play *the* leading role in its development, with the establishment of the RAF College. The army had Sandhurst, the navy had Dartmouth and the RAF would have Cranwell.

Cranwell had already fulfilled a training role in the First World War, when Royal Naval Air Service training facilities for seaplanes, balloons and airships was centralised here. The first new RAF two-year cadet course began in February 1920, and many soon-to-be famous names passed through its hands. Such was the need for new pilots that additional Flying Training Schools were opened, together with dedicated bases for armaments training. In addition, by the early 1930s, with the reassertion of German militarism, plans had to be laid for the provision of state-of-the-art operational bases. Once again, Lincolnshire's proximity to mainland Europe meant that the county would take much of the strain.

The architectural merit of the airfields of the expansion years cannot be denied. Neo-Georgian in style, with input from architects such as Sir Edwin Lutyens, they were intended to be permanent additions to the landscape. An imposing main gate, flanked by a guardroom, led to a Station HQ. Feeder roads leading off to left and right culminated in a centrally located barrack square. This would be surrounded by barrack blocks, NAAFI and Airmen's and Sergeants' Mess buildings. The Officers' Mess was usually set off at a distance. Also set apart, towards the runways, was the Technical Site with a wide variety of workshops and, of course, hangars – usually three in number. The latter were 'C Types', brick-built with trademark sliding doors. The most exposed structure, perched on the edge of the Technical Site, was the Control Tower, or 'Watch Office'.

As might be expected, construction was a slow process. By 1940, only half-a-dozen of the bases had actually been completed in Lincolnshire. These were: Scampton, Waddington, Hemswell, Kirton-in-Lindsey, Manby and Digby. At the time of writing (2015) the infrastructure of all of these remains largely intact.

While a lot of thought went into airfield design, there was a distinct lack of foresight when it came to utility. For example, grass was the preferred choice of material for the runways. When the heavy bombers eventually came on line, turning grass runways into quagmires, concrete runways had to be hastily constructed. Similarly, although ample use was made of reinforced concrete, it became apparent that having everything and everybody so tightly packed together could work to the advantage of enemy bombers.

On the declaration of war, on 3rd September 1939, many airfields remained uncompleted, and corners had to be cut in an effort to get them ready for action. It was recognised that these 'designer' airfields would be insufficient and that more would be needed.

In the 1930s, getting the land for building airfields had proved difficult, but, with the country on a war footing, land could be acquired far more easily. Occasionally, for instance, a Lincolnshire farmer would find out that his land had been requisitioned only when the bulldozers appeared. Sometimes, things were different, provided one knew the right people. When the Air Ministry wanted to take the house and grounds of Gunby Hall for inclusion in a new Bomber Command base (RAF Spilsby), the estate's owners – the Massingberd family – successfully appealed to King George VI, and the proposed site was shifted to the south-west.

The new, rapidly constructed wartime airfields were never intended to be permanent additions to the landscape. The most enduring features were the new concrete runways. The standard arrangement was for three intersecting lengths: a main runway of 2,000 yards in length and two secondary runways, each 1,400 yards long – the layout being enclosed by a perimeter track, branching off which were 'hard standings', or parking areas for aircraft. Individual hangars could also be situated along the course of the perimeter track. The most popular wartime design was the 'T2'. Steel-framed and clad with corrugated iron, it was mass produced and easily erected and dismantled.

Domestic facilities were dispersed over perhaps half a dozen additional sites away from the main airfield. It was here that many of the temporary semi-circular, corrugated iron Nissen huts and brick, cement-coated Maycrete structures one associates with Second World War airfields were to be found. Catering for the needs of two thousand RAF personnel often led to the creation of communities that dwarfed the villages to which they were attached, with airfields having their own churches, post offices and even cinemas. They also had their own sewage plants – still used by Anglian Water – and may be credited with introducing modern plumbing to rural Lincolnshire.

In total, bombers flew from some 26 airfields spread throughout Lincolnshire. Fighter Command airfields, although fewer in number, were essential for defence. Minimalist in design, they were far easier to set up. Lincolnshire's main fighter station was RAF Digby which was, perhaps unfairly, considered a quiet spot, to which Battle of Britain pilots were posted for recuperation. There were two Coastal Command airfields – at North Coates and Strubby – and, of course, there were the American bases, at Goxhill, Folkingham, Fulbeck, North Witham and Barkston Heath.

But what of the aircraft that flew from these bases? Unlike the fighters that were coming into production, the bombers of the early years of the war left a lot to be desired. The single-engine Fairey Battle light bomber, for example, first flew in 1936. Slow and lightly-armed, it was withdrawn front front-line service by the end of 1940. The Bristol Blenheim dated from 1935. A twin-engine fighter-bomber, it took heavy punishment in its fighter role in the Battle of Britain. As a bomber, it fared little better, occasionally suffering 100% losses during missions.

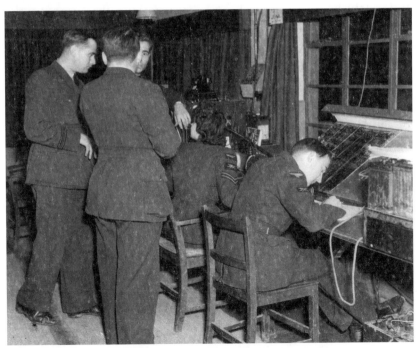

Inside the Control Tower, RAF Fiskerton, January 1944. (ww2images)

The Handley Page Hampden, immediately recognisable by its very narrow fuselage, represented something of a step in the right direction. It looked more like a long-range bomber and pilots thought that it handled well, but the interior was cramped and, most tellingly, it was armed with only two machine guns, rendering it, once again, vulnerable to enemy fighter attacks. The Vickers Wellington was a far more formidable proposition. It was more powerful – having two 1,500 hp engines, in contrast to the Hampden's 1,000 hp engines – and heavily armed, with eight machine guns: two in the nose, four in the tail and two in beam positions.

The most iconic bomber of the Second World War – the Avro Lancaster – officially entered service in 1942, with 44 Squadron, based at RAF Waddington. On 3rd/4th March that year, four Lancasters were despatched on a mine laying mission on the north-western coast of Germany. Facilities for aircrew were rather restricted, but an expansive bomb bay gave it a bomb load capacity far exceeding that of any of its predecessors.

The Supermarine Spitfire, operating from Lincolnshire's handful of fighter airfields, was not always a pilot's preferred choice. Its handling and performance were outstanding, and it should be remembered that R. J. Mitchell's design appeared at a time when the RAF was not looking far beyond the biplane as a future tool of war in the air. However, the Spitfire's great rival, the Hawker Hurricane, although heavier and slower, had better manoeuvrability and greater stability.

One of the most exciting new aircraft to appear during the war years was the de Havilland Mosquito fighter-bomber. Fast and manoeuvrable, the mosquitoes had the capability of making precision low-level raids. Their two Rolls Royce Merlin engines gave them a speed of 360 mph, enabling them to outrun German fighters. They were so fast that, initially, the designers – who envisaged it as a reconnaissance vehicle – saw no need to include cannon or machine guns.

In terms of unsung heroes of the air, the Airspeed Oxford must rank highly. A twin-engine training aircraft, the Oxford was developed by the Airspeed company to fulfil all the RAF's needs. Pilots, navigators, radio operators, bomb aimers and gunners all honed their skills on the Oxford which became a familiar sight in the skies over Lincolnshire. Airspeed also produced the Horsa glider. Constructed of wood, the Horsa came in several component parts to be assembled by sub-contracted furniture manufacturers. It was the RAF's main glider and, as such, was deployed during the D-Day landings and at Arnhem.

The Americans brought their own aircraft. The first British RAF airfield to be occupied by them was Goxhill. In June, 1942, General Eisenhower attended a special ceremony to mark the occasion. Shortly before his arrival, in what can hardly have been a coincidence, Goxhill was bombed for the first and only time during the entire war. In the hands of the United States 8th Army Air Force, the base was used for the training of pilots for the Lockheed P-38 'Lightning' twin-engine fighter-bomber. The young Americans enjoyed taking risks in the air, and there were more than 50 crashes, resulting in 23 deaths.

The remaining American bases in Lincolnshire were occupied by the Troop Carrier Groups of the 9th Army Air Force, to concentrate on the transport of men and materials. The primary vehicle for this task was the Douglas C-47. It was essentially the Douglas DC-3 passenger airliner with the seats taken out. More familiarly known as the 'Skytrain', it became famous for its ability to take punishment and remain in the air.

The 9th played an essential supporting role in 'Operation Overlord' – the D-Day landings. The Troop Carrier Command Pathfinder Group at North Witham had the task of parachuting in ahead of the main airborne divisions and marking the drop sites with radar beacons. The 82nd Airborne Division subsequently took off from Fulbeck for its drop zone near Saint-Mere-Eglise. During the drop, Private John Steele's parachute famously got caught on the spire of the town church, and he remained suspended there while the fight for the town continued. The incident was later faithfully reproduced in the film *The Longest Day*.

A far less satisfactory expedition was 'Operation Market Garden', which was launched on 17th September 1944. A British idea to bring a speedy conclusion to the war by invading Germany via Holland, it ended in tragedy. The plan depended on complete surprise to overwhelm the retreating German forces. Once more, however, German intelligence was not left wanting and Panzer divisions were waiting at key crossings of the Rhine, at Eindhoven and Arnhem. Skytrains, often towing gliders, delivered the troops and followed up with supply drops, but after a week, the operation had to be abandoned.

In the early months of 1945, the Americans vacated their Lincolnshire bases, moving on to forward airfields in France. They were sadly missed. Their generosity towards the local population was legendary, building up a rapport which has endured for seventy years.

It should not be forgotten that the Americans were only one of many nationalities that could be found on Lincolnshire's airfields. The countries of the old British Empire – Canada, Australia, New Zealand, the Caribbean and South African – were well represented, as were the free forces of occupied Europe representing, among others, France, Norway, Poland and Czechoslovakia.

British RAF service personnel who were sent to Lincolnshire hated it. Talking about RAF Scampton, Guy Gibson observed: 'Sunny Scampton we call it because it's in Lincolnshire and one doesn't see much sun up there.' Gibson did not think much of RAF Digby, either: 'Here Lincolnshire is at its worst – a vast area of flatness, spreading out towards the East Fenlands of the Wash.' The pet names aircrew gave to their airfields summed up the feeling: Goxhill was 'Goathill'; Ludford Magna became 'Mudford Magna'; Sandtoft was 'Prangtoft'. And wasn't it true that ex-Chief of the Air Staff, Hugh Trenchard, had selected Cranwell as the site of

Guy Gibson VC (Author's collection)

the RAF training college because it was 'marooned in the wilderness' and, as such, offered little to distract cadets from their studies?

Perhaps it was just being away from home that was the problem, but it certainly did not stop them from doing their duty – and quite often going way beyond their duty. The truth was that acts of heroism became almost routine. A total of 23 Victoria Crosses was awarded to Bomber Command aircrew. Whenever a Lancaster bomber was shot down, it took with it a complement of seven men: pilot, flight engineer, navigator, wireless operator, bomb aimer, mid-upper gunner and rear gunner. More than 25,000 lost their lives between 1939 and 1945. Counting the injured and POWs, the total casualty rate was 70%. (Remarkably, only one wartime Fighter Command pilot won the Victoria Cross. He was James Brindley Nicholson, who subsequently became 1459 Flight's CO at RAF Hibaldstow.)

Little wonder that aircrews were notoriously superstitious. An aircraft thought to be unlucky would be deliberately ditched. Similarly, it might be noticed that aircrew who failed to return from operations happened to have dated a particular WAAF, and from then on, the girl would be shunned. Good luck charms and mascots were without number. One of the most unusual superstitions was 50 Squadron's insistence upon listening to a record of the Andrews Sisters singing 'The Shrine of St Cecilia' before setting out on a mission.

To relieve the tension, the Americans could look forward to visits from the Glenn Miller Orchestra. On a smaller scale, the budding entertainer, Max Bygraves, stationed at RAF North Coates, devised a revue appropriately entitled 'Chocks Away'. Another future famous name, Michael Bentine, founder member of The Goons, served at RAF Wickenby. And celebrated actor Donald Pleasence, flew with 166 Squadron from RAF Kirmington. Shot down over Agenville on 31st August 1944, he became a prisoner of war. One of his best known films would be *The Great Escape* – in which, fittingly, he played an RAF Officer POW.

Pleasence was shot down during a daytime raid and, throughout the war years, bombing missions were mounted around the clock. As a rule, the daytime missions were minor affairs, carried out by a few aircraft – often Mosquitoes. The heavy raids were carried out under cover of darkness involving, until 1942, an average of 100 aircraft.

From the beginning of 1942, Bomber Command was led by Air Chief Marshal Sir Arthur 'Bomber' Harris. He did not invent the concept of blanket bombing, which may have originated with the grandees of the RAF, who remembered the devastating effect of the Zeppelin raids upon civilian morale twenty five years earlier

The Dambusters memorial, in the shape of a breached dam, in Royal Square Gardens, Woodhall Spa

– but he did believe that the war could be won by bombing alone.

The first of Harris's famous 1,000 bomber raids took place on the night of 30th-31st May 1942 and was directed against Cologne. The raid did considerable damage, and up to a quarter of the civilian population fled the city. RAF casualties were also high, with the loss of 41 aircraft. One of the latter was flown by Flight Lieutenant Leslie Manser. His Avro Manchester from RAF Skellingthorpe was hit by flak over the target and got as far as Holland on the return leg when it began to lose height. Manser told the crew to bail out, while he himself remained at the controls. The aircraft exploded and Manser was killed – his actions earning the 20-year-old pilot a posthumous Victoria Cross.

Bomber Command has earned much opprobrium for its attempts to pound Germany into submission by directly targeting the civilian populations of its major cities. The first of the devastating firestorms caused by concentrated bombing occurred in Hamburg on the night of 27th-28th July 1943, and resulted in the deaths of 40,000 citizens. At least 12,000 were killed in a raid on Darmstadt

The Petwood, Woodhall Spa, officers' mess for 617 Squadron, 1943-1945

on 11th-12th September 1944, while up to 50,000 lives were lost in Dresden on 13th-14th February 1945.

Precision raids on industrial targets were a far more difficult proposition. They could be expensive in terms of numbers of aircraft lost, while accuracy left a lot to be desired – although it was improved by the creation of an elite 'Pathfinder' force, to fly ahead and identify and mark targets. Thus, while a raid on the V-2 rocket site at Peenemunde on 17th-18th August 1943 was very successful, 40 aircraft were brought down. Prime targets throughout the war included Essen, with its Krupp armaments factory; Kiel, centre of U-boat production, and Schweinfurt, chief manufactory of ball bearings. Inevitably, civilian casualties were sustained – as, indeed, they were in the London 'Blitz', Coventry, Plymouth, Hull and in many other British towns and cities.

By far the most celebrated precision attack was that carried out by the newly formed 617 Squadron on the night of 16th-17th May 1943. It involved the crews of 19 Lancasters in six weeks of intensive training, designed to ensure that they could drop a very special type of bomb: a 'bouncing bomb'. Developed by aircraft designer Barnes Wallis, the bomb was shaped like a large oil drum, 11 feet in diameter and weighed 10 tons. Dropped onto water from a height of 60 feet, it would bounce along the surface before hitting its intended target – the wall of a dam. The aim of what was called 'Operation Chastise' was to disable the industry of the Ruhr Valley by disrupting its water supply, through knocking out three dams: the Mohne, Eder and Sorpe. The raid was scheduled for May so that advantage could be taken of high water levels following the spring rains. For maximum effect, the water had to be no lower than four feet from the top of the dams. The operation's leader, Wing Commander Guy Gibson, prepared his crews with the aid of Lincolnshire's canal system, flying along the waterways at night until correct heights and speeds were achieved.

The attack force, flying from RAF Scampton, was divided into three formations. Gibson himself led the assault on the

Mohne and Eder; a second formation made for the Sorpe, while a third followed up in reserve. Although it took several attempts, the Mohne was breached, and Gibson flew on to the Eder. This, too, was breached – with the last available bomb. The simultaneous attack on the Sorpe failed. With this dam still functioning, industrial production was not disrupted as much might otherwise have been the case. Nevertheless, 'Operation Chastise' was an outstanding achievement and a great morale booster. The price of success was a heavy one: a total of eight Lancasters and 53 lives were lost – flak over the targets being very heavy. This would be expected in such sensitive locations and the enterprise had been planned in great secrecy, but German knowledge about British airfields and their operations was often uncomfortably accurate. A few unguarded words uttered in the wrong place at the wrong time could have been enough to put the enemy on his guard.

Gibson was awarded the Victoria Cross for his part in the raid. Sadly, he did not survive the war. Flying his 627 Squadron Mosquito from RAF Coningsby he was lost on 19th–20th September 1944, following a raid on Mönchengladbach. Gibson's old squadron, 617, led for a time by Group Captain Leonard Cheshire, went from strength to strength. In November 1944, in tandem with 9 Squadron from RAF Bardney, it sank the German battleship Tirpitz, at anchor near Troms. On 14th March 1945, it was chosen to drop the first 22,000lb 'Grand Slam' bomb in a raid that destroyed the Bielefeld railway viaduct.

Bomber Command operations continued until May 1945. One of the last missions involved an attack on Berchtesgaden, Hitler's 'Eagle's Nest'. Two Lancasters were shot down in what was really a vanity project.

Essential work included missions to fly home 75,000 POWs and 'Operation Manna', comprising food drops to the starving inhabitants of the Netherlands.

As the war ended, a new long-range bomber to replace the Lancaster was in production. This was the Avro Lincoln – bigger,

The Commonwealth War Graves Commission site in Scopwick Church Burial Ground includes 50 headstones commemorating Commonwealth aircrew- mainly Canadians associated with RAF Digby

heavier and faster, and intended to be a leading component of 'Tiger Force', destined for the Pacific and the fight against Japan. During trials, it was discovered that it would not fit into the standard 'T2' hangar, owing to its increased wingspan. At RAF Kelstern, the problem was tackled by sinking tramlines into the concrete, setting the Lincoln on a trolley and pushing it in sideways. (Kelstern's 'T2' has gone, but the tramlines are still there.)

With the surrender of Japan, the war was really over. The men and women of the RAF, the aircraft and the airfields were no longer needed. The airfields of the pre-war expansion period were retained, but the temporary bases were either closed immediately or, at best, mothballed, to be returned to agricultural use within a few years.

The presence of RAF Care & Maintenance personnel on the mothballed sites did nothing to deter squatters moving in, for the post-war years were a time of acute housing shortage. At RAF Sandtoft, coal mining families occupied some of the buildings, and each day the miners would cycle the eight miles to work at Thorne colliery.

Particularly sought after as accommodation were the abandoned control towers, especially the earlier models which had plenty of picture-windows. (Later designs, taking into account much shattering of plate-glass during air-raids, made more generous use of brick.) A number are still in use as domestic dwellings – although rather more luxurious – notably at Sandtoft, Strubby and Hibaldstowe.

Sometimes, the accommodation, rough and ready though might be, was used officially. Until 1948, for example, RAF Ludford Magna served as a transit camp for Polish refugees. Other stations, such as RAF Wellingore, served as POW camps for Germans who were put to work on local farms.

Other airfields found more exciting employment. The USAAF base at Folkingham was used by Raymond Mays (see page 196) as a testing ground for British Racing Motors (BRM). For a time, Folkingham seemed to be ideally placed to become the home of motor racing in Britain, but the prize eventually went to another old airfield: Silverstone in Northamptonshire. Apart from a temporary absence, BRM used Folkingham until the mid-1960s, by which time a new war was raging, one that had begun even before the Second World War was over: the Cold War between East and West.

Following the defeat of Germany, Berlin had been divided into four zones, controlled by the USSR, USA, France and Britain. In June 1948, the USSR cut off land and water routes in and out of the war torn city, leaving the western sectors with just over a month's supply of food and coal. The only way in was by air,

Avro Lancaster R5689 of 50 Squadron, written off when it crash-landed on its return to base - RAF Swinderby - on 19th September 1942. (1000aircraftphotos.com)

and the USAAF, supported by the RAF, took on the seemingly impossible task of flying in 5,000 tons of supplies per day from airfields in West Germany. The Americans mainly used C-47 Skytrains, while the RAF scraped up every available aircraft, including Short Sunderland flying boats. The targets were reached, with the airlift continuing for a year before the USSR relented and re-opened communications.

During the airlift, USAAF B-29 bombers had moved into RAF Waddington and RAF Scampton, and Britain was now the last line of defence against Soviet aggression. This thinking was still prevalent in 1959 when, as part of 'Project Emily', six wartime Lincolnshire airfields were selected to house American Thor Intermediate Range Ballistic Missiles. RAF Hemswell was one of four main Thor bases in the UK, and had four satellite bases: RAF Bardney, RAF Caistor, RAF Coleby Grange and RAF Ludford Magna. Each had three IRBM launchers armed with 1.44 megaton thermonuclear warheads. (The same arrangement applied to RAF Folkingham, which was commanded from RAF North Luffenham.) While the bases themselves were administered by the RAF, American personnel were present to control the launches, should it ever become necessary. Briefly, in 1962, it looked as though it would become necessary when the Cuban Missile Crisis nudged the world towards a nuclear catastrophe.

Undoubtedly, there were occasions when accidents nearly resulted in disaster. It has come to light that in December 1960, an attempt to fuel one of the missiles at RAF Ludford Magna resulted in a tank load of liquid oxygen being emptied in error onto the launch pad. One cannot help wondering if this was an isolated incident. Perhaps it is better not to know.

In any event, the missile sites were dismantled in 1963, but evidence of their existence can still be seen in the indestructible concrete launch pads and blast walls. With the exception of RAF Hemswell (a pre-war expansion station) much of the wartime infrastructure of the Thor base sites was destroyed in

The sites of most Lincolnshire Bomber Command airfields have squadron memorials. This one, commemorating aircrew of 57 and 630 Squadrons who lost their lives, is at the entrance to the Lincolnshire Aviation Heritage Centre, East Kirkby

the process of their conversion.

Abandoned airfields can be a sorry sight, but what is to be done with them? Of those that have been returned to farming, many have runways and/or perimeter tracks that are still intact. It has been easier to leave them *in situ* than to make the Herculean effort required to dig them up. Alternatively, the wealth of available hardcore has led to the metamorphosis of some old bases into industrial estates and housing developments. RAF Skellingthorpe is now the Birchwood residential suburb of Lincoln, while RAF Swinderby has been transformed into the community of Witham St. Hughes.

Industrial development has not always led to the complete erasure of an airfield from the Lincolnshire landscape. Both RAF Faldingworth and RAF Fiskerton have been used by manufacturers of armaments and ammunition, who have left the infrastructure undisturbed. Surviving features of Bomber Command airfields include wartime firing range butts – substantial walls of red brick. The facility at Fiskerton is still used to test the ammunition manufactured on site.

Defunct expansion period airfields present a different problem. Given the architectural merit of many of the buildings, it is not quite so simple to raze them to the ground. Perhaps there is no need for such drastic action. A portion of RAF Hemswell became the village of Hemswell Cliff, but original structures on the main site have been developed into shops for the sale of antiques; the Station HQ is now the Blenheim Care Centre, and the Officers' Mess is the Hemswell Court Hotel. The Control Tower has been adapted for trading and one of the magnificent 'C' hangars is used to accommodate a Sunday 'flea market'. With a little thought, the old and the new can live side by side.

A not dissimilar arrangement can be found at RAF Binbrook. Both these sites have also been used for filming: Hemswell for *The Dambusters* (1955) and Binbrook for *Memphis Belle* (1990). Another old airfield in demand with film units (with credits which include *Doctor Who*) is USAAF North Witham. After the war, this base was developed into woodland and is now a butterfly reserve – surely the most unusual transformation of all.

RAF Coningsby is the only Lincolnshire airfield still fully functioning as a bomber station, but there are still many stretches of surviving wartime runway in the county where, in the stillness of a summer's evening, it is easy to imagine the sights and sounds of an active wartime airfield: ground-crews urgently readying aircraft for take-off; the bustling interior of the control tower as WAAFs prepare for their nightly vigil, and the roar of Rolls Royce engines as, for one last time, the Lancaster squadrons of Bomber County reach for the sky.

Chapter Twelve

SCIENTIFIC LINCOLNSHIRE

Sir Isaac Newton

The man who has been described as the greatest genius who ever lived was born in 1642, in the Lincolnshire hamlet of Woolsthorpe-by-Colsterworth. His early education at The King's School, Grantham was of limited value to a boy of his turn of mind for, although Latin was on the curriculum, mathematics was not. His real interests found expression in hobbies such as model-making, resulting in the construction of model windmills, paper lanterns, kites and sundials.

He was removed from school temporarily, to work on his parents' farm, his duties including sale of the farm produce at Grantham's Saturday market. Nevertheless, encouraged by Henry Stokes, headmaster of The King's School and an uncle, William Ayscough, Rector of Burton Coggles, he eventually found his way to Trinity College, Cambridge. Here, he formulated many of the groundbreaking theories which he would spend many years developing.

In 1665, the Great Plague forced Cambridge to close for a time. It was during his enforced absence that the famous incident of the falling apple occurred. It was later described by William Stukeley (see page 145) in his *Memoirs of Sir Isaac Newton's Life*.

According to Stukeley, Newton had been sitting in the garden at Woolsthorpe, under the shade of an apple tree, when he began to muse on the reason why apples should always 'descend perpendicularly' to the ground, as opposed to moving upwards or sideways. This simple observation led him to wonder whether the force that governed the behaviour of the apple could also be responsible for keeping the Moon in its settled orbit around the Earth.

It is almost easier to identify the areas of science which Newton did *not* study than to list those to which he made significant contributions. His studies of light showed that white light is made up of different colours, and the way in which it can be divided into colours of the spectrum. His work in astronomy included the construction of both reflecting and refracting telescopes – both of which he cobbled together for his own amusement, in much the same way that he had made his models as a schoolboy. His great mathematical discovery was the differential calculus.

Newton's three-volume *Philosophiae Naturalis Principia Mathematica*, in which he set out his major ideas, was published in 1686-87. When it came to publishing his findings, he always displayed a curious reticence. The modern scientist, supported by well-staffed laboratories, is eager to get into print and to reap the benefits of his/her research. For Newton, working independently, the 'finished product' was sufficient reward in itself. That the *Principia* found its way into print when it did was thanks largely to the personal efforts of the astronomer, Edmund Halley. An aversion to publicising one's work, however, can result in many difficulties. For example, in 1677, when Newton's rooms caught fire, irreplaceable unpublished records and manuscripts were lost for ever. It can also lead to conflict with one's rivals, as Newton found when the German Gottfried von Leibniz claimed to have beaten him to the mark in his calculus work – the 'Leibniz-Newton controversy'.

In 1696, he made what many thought to be the astonishing decision to turn his back on Cambridge and abandon academic life. He moved to London, where he took up the post of Warden of the Royal Mint, becoming Master of the Royal Mint three years later.

The Mint was in the process of replacing all the coins in circulation owing, in part, to the ease with which the old, worn-out coins could be counterfeited. Newton's arrival was fortunate for the health of the economy, for he approached the tasks which lay ahead of him with all his customary vigour and commitment. His mathematical skills were put to good use, but he also went undercover to weed out the counterfeiters, donning disguises to enable him to mix freely with members of the underworld in seedy taverns.

In 1705, Newton was knighted. He never married and spent his declining years living with his niece. His outstanding work at the Royal Mint was not mirrored in his management of his own financial affairs. Generous to a fault where his relatives were concerned, he also invested heavily in 'South Sea Bubble' ventures – worthless companies formed to attract speculators – and is reputed to have lost £20,000.

Sir Isaac Newton was born at Woolsthorpe, 8 miles from Grantham, but he attended The King's School in the town- a sufficiently strong connection to justify this statue in the town centre

Newton died on 20th March 1727 at the age of 84 and was buried in Westminster Abbey. His childhood home, Woolsthorpe Manor is now a hands-on museum, run by the National Trust. The famous apple tree is still there, albeit having been re-rooted on a number of occasions. Major Tim Peake's 2015-16 mission to the International Space Station was named *Principiae*, in honour of Newton's famous work. Peake even took along some seeds from the fruit of the tree. While Newton would have been intrigued by the science of space travel, his response to the apple seed stunt may have been a little more guarded.

Sir Joseph Banks

The naturalist, Joseph Banks was born in London, but in 1743, when he was two years old, his father inherited Revesby Abbey in Lincolnshire, and Revesby became the family home.

Joseph eventually went to Eton, but the time he spent roaming the Lincolnshire countryside, exploring the rich diversity of its plant and animal life, shaped his destiny. He went on to Christ Church, Oxford, but found it little to his taste because his favourite subject, botany, was largely ignored. His father died in 1761 and, when he attained his majority, Joseph Banks took over management of the Revesby estate. Anyone else might have been content to settle into the leisurely life of a country squire, but, while he never neglected his domestic responsibilities, Banks was keen to develop his understanding of the natural world.

In 1766, he set out on his first journey of exploration, abroad the frigate, HMS *Niger,* bound for Newfoundland and Labrador on naval business. It was a valuable formative experience for Banks, who was able to collect examples of plant and marine life. Perhaps most important of all, however, during his time in Newfoundland, he met Lieutenant James Cook.

Two years later, Banks was ready for the adventure of a lifetime. This time, he sailed not on a warship, but on a collier especially adapted for a scientific voyage. The professed objective was to observe the Transit of Venus from Tahiti, but the real purpose was to locate the continent of Australia – 'Terra Australis Incognita'. HMS *Endeavour,* commanded by James Cook, set sail from Plymouth in August 1768. The vessel reached Brazil in November, putting in at Rio de Janeiro and then Tierra del Fuego. From here, they set off for Tahiti, from where the astronomical observations were to be made. They arrived on 13 April 1769, in good time for the Transit of Venus across the Sun which would occur in early June. This provided Banks and his team with ample opportunity to collect examples of flora and fauna. Banks himself even managed to master the native language.

The official task completed, they sailed on in search of the Southern Continent. On 6th October 1769, they sighted New Zealand – first encountered by Abel Tasman in 1642. They found the Maoris to be particularly pugnacious. However, Banks was able to communicate with them, and it must have been frustrating for him when Cook quite rightly decided it was too risky to stay. Exploration was therefore limited to the coastline, although during brief excursions ashore, Banks was able to add to his collection of specimens.

Sailing on, they sighted the eastern coastline of Australia on 19 April 1770. A week later, they landed at an inlet, later to be known as Botany Bay in honour of Banks. Here, contact was made with the Aborigines, who ran off when muskets were fired at them. After allowing time for Banks to do some work, Cook proceeded north, only for *Endeavour* to be holed on the Great Barrier Reef. This was a lucky break for Banks, for Cook had to put into an estuary (Endeavour River) to make temporary repairs, enabling him to add to his burgeoning collection. Under way once more, *Endeavour* passed around the tip of Cape York Peninsula, pressing on through Torres Strait. Cook claimed the whole of the coastline he had explored for the British Crown.

The journey home was not without its difficulties. Cook prided himself that not one crew member had succumbed to scurvy, but he put into Jakarta in the Dutch East Indies to complete repairs. Here, many of his men caught malaria. Twenty of them expired, together with three of Banks's team, including his artists John Reynolds and Sydney Parkinson. When the survivors eventually docked at Deal on 12 July 1771, they learned that they had all long since been given up for dead.

Banks planned to accompany Cook on his second voyage to Australia in 1772, but his requirements included the provision of additional upper decks which made the vessel, HMS *Resolution*, top heavy. He seemed unable to appreciate that his demands rendered the ship unseaworthy and, rather churlishly, refused to compromise. The Admiralty replaced him with another botanist,

Deer on the Revesby Abbey Estate, home of Sir Joseph Banks

Johann Forster. Unfortunately, Forster did not have Banks's financial advantages and when he returned from the voyage, he was forced to sell the illustrations which had been painstakingly created by his son. Banks bought the lot.

Perhaps Banks had changed his mind about undertaking another arduous voyage so soon after the first. He had brought back an enormous amount of material: domestic utensils, tools, weapons, costumes, plants, insects, preserved animals, fish and birds – the list is almost endless. He used his London house in New Burlington Street to display as much as he could and began the daunting task of cataloguing it all.

When it came to publishing accounts of his discoveries, Banks met with little initial success. His journals, along with those of Cook, had been turned over to the Admiralty and resulted in a couple of disappointing volumes, hastily thrown together. He did embark upon the compilation of a colossal florilegium, using his artists' drawings and involving the production of over 700 copper plates, but the production costs got out of hand, and he had to abandon the project. (A limited edition of 35 volumes was finally published in the 1980s.)

Joseph Banks made only one more voyage – to Iceland in 1772, after which he spent much of his time promoting the study of his beloved botany. In 1781, he was knighted by George III, with whom he became friendly, and became involved in the development of the Royal Gardens at Kew Palace.

A more controversial aspect of his later career concerned his interest in the settlement of Australia and, in particular, his proposals to use Botany Bay as a penal colony. He argued that the community would be self-supporting and, as the indigenous population was nomadic, there would no need to compensate anyone for taking possession of the land.

Sir Joseph Banks died in 1820. Although the Revesby estate is not accessible to the public, a lay-by on the A155 has an information panel providing an outline of his work. Descendants of the deer and merino sheep he introduced can be seen grazing in the park. Visitors to Horncastle will be familiar with the town's Sir Joseph Banks Centre, aimed at celebrating his life and work, while the Sir Joseph Banks Conservatory at The Lawn in Lincoln commemorates the plants he discovered on his ground-breaking voyages of discovery.

William Stukeley

Dr. Johnson defines an *antiquary* as 'a man studious of antiquity; a collector of ancient things'. During the eighteenth century, antiquaries, although amateurs in their field of interest, were academically quite respectable. In later years, their standing declined, the discipline of archaeology – which they had done so much to foster – regarding them as interfering busybodies, much as people who use metal detectors are frowned upon today.

Lincolnshire accommodated many individuals of antiquarian pursuits, particular among village clergymen, who often had time on their hands. One example is the Reverend Cayley Illingworth. Actually, he enjoyed little free time, for he was Archdeacon of Stowe, Vicar of Stainton and Rector of Scampton and Epworth. Had it not been for his ecclesiastical commitments, he would have undertaken far more archaeological work. He is best known for the discovery and excavation of a Roman villa at Scampton. In 1810, he published his findings in a work illustrated by William Fowler of Winterton, another antiquarian who used his skills as a draughtsman to excellent effect.

The county's most celebrated antiquary was William Stukeley who was born in Holbeach in 1687. He attended the Free School in Holbeach and went on to study medicine via Corpus Christi College, Cambridge and St. Thomas' Hospital. He established his first practice in 1710, in Boston, remaining there for seven years when, tiring of 'dirty roads and dull company', he moved to London. In middle age, he began to suffer from gout, which made it increasingly difficult for him to follow his profession and, in 1726, he retired to Grantham, to marry 'a lady of good family and fortune'. Nevertheless, he decided to take Holy Orders. In 1730, he was presented to the living of the parish of All Saints, Stamford, to which was added in 1739 the living of Somerby. In 1729, he left Lincolnshire for ever, to take up the appointment of Rector of the Church of St. George the Martyr in Bloomsbury, where he remained until his death in 1765.

Stukeley is best known for his work entitled *Stonehenge and Avebury*, published in 1743. His attempts to date Stonehenge were wide of the mark. He thought it was completed around 460BC, whereas it is now thought to date from 3000BC. He also postulated that both Stonehenge and Avebury had strong Druidical connections.

In the late 1740s, he was duped by the literary forgery, *Descriptions of Britain*, allegedly written by an English monk of the fifteenth century, but actually forged by a man called Charles Bertram. Stukeley was instrumental in establishing the 'authenticity' of the manuscript, which became accepted as a major source of information about Roman Britain.

Stukeley was a great frequenter of societies of one kind or another. He became a Freemason and was a founder member of the Egyptian Society, a short-lived venture which, despite being steeped in odd rituals, had a well-meaning aim of promoting interest in Egyptian antiquities. Other societies included the Gentleman's Society of Spalding, aimed at promoting 'useful learning … and the knowledge of antiquities and nature', and the 'Brazen Nose Society' – Stukeley's attempt to establish something along the same lines as the Gentleman's Society in Stamford.

He was the first Secretary of the Society of Antiquaries, formed in 1718, although he preferred attending meetings of the Royal Society, of which he had become a Fellow a year earlier.

It was at the instigation of the Duke of Montagu, whom he had met through the Egyptian Society that Stukeley left Stamford for London. The move was not effected without regret. 'I leave', he said, 'a most elegant place … it is as pretty a seat as ever I saw.' He is referring to his house in Barn Hill and, in particular, to the garden which he spent years creating. It included a hermitage – a popular feature of formal gardens at that time – a Temple of Flora and a Temple of Bacchus. The man to whom he sold the house, a Mr. Noel, pulled it all down.

One of his interests was earthquakes, of which he made a study. Writing of minor earthquakes he had witnessed in London, he says he was 'perceptible of it at the first, and began then to perceive the cause … it was certainly an electrical vibration, and nothing under the earth caused it.' He was openly critical of Fellows of the Royal Society for providing only 'circumstantial descriptions' of earthquakes without making any attempt to explain their cause.

Stukeley's theories about many things may have been fanciful, but he was a pioneer in the clinical study of ancient monuments. In this respect, he was an accurate observer and recorder of all that he saw – the illustrations accompanying his studies of Stonehenge and Avebury providing an invaluable record of what these monuments looked like during his lifetime, prior to damage inflicted by future generations.

Chapter Thirteen

LITERARY LINCOLNSHIRE

Alfred, Lord Tennyson

Lincolnshire's most celebrated poet was born in the hamlet of Somersby in 1809. His father was Rector of St. Margaret's Church and Alfred, one of eleven children, was raised in an extended cottage which served as the rectory. His fame in later life attracted many back-dated anecdotes about his childhood, such as his prodigious physical strength which he displayed by carrying a Shetland pony around the garden and beating the brawny village youths in raucous games. He received his early schooling at Louth Grammar School – where he was usually on the receiving end of thrashings from schoolmasters and bullying from fellow pupils.

In 1827, he went up to Cambridge, where he published his first collection of poems and where he also met Arthur Hallam who became his closest friend. When Tennyson's father died, in 1831, he had to return to Somersby without taking his degree. The family were allowed to stay on at the rectory for a time and Hallam, who had become engaged to Tennyson's sister, Emily, was a regular visitor.

The year 1833 was one of the worst in Tennyson's long life. His second book of poems (which included *The Lady of Shalott, The Lotus Eaters* and *Morte d'Arthur*) was savaged by the critics, as a result of which he wrote nothing for ten years. To compound his woes,

Hallam died suddenly. When the family had to leave the rectory, Tennyson embarked upon an itinerant lifestyle, dividing his time between the new family home in Cheltenham and sojourns with friends. His situation was not improved by the fact that he had lost most of the money he did have by investing it in a dubious business venture. Fortunately, a new volume of poems, which included *Locksley Hall* and *Ulysses*, proved a commercial success. In addition, he was awarded an annual Civil List pension of £200.

In 1850 Tennyson published *In Memoriam A.H.H.*, his tribute to Arthur Hallam, and succeeded William Wordsworth as Poet

Statue of Tennyson with his Russian Wolfhound, Karenina, on the East Green of Lincoln Cathedral

Laureate. He also married his long-time love, Emily, the niece of Sir John Franklin (see page 111) and, in 1853, rented (and later purchased) a house called 'Farringford' on the Isle of Wight. In 1853, he wrote what became arguably his most popular poem, *The Charge of the Light Brigade.*

Tennyson's success enabled him to build a mansion, 'Aldworth', in Sussex and he moved there in 1869, keeping 'Farringford' as a holiday home. In 1884, he was created Baron Tennyson of Aldworth. He continued writing to the end of his life. He was 70 when he wrote *The Revenge* and 80 years of age when he penned *Crossing the Bar.*

While Tennyson paid occasional visits to Lincolnshire, he never returned to Somersby.

And yet, the county continued to exert a strong influence on his poetry. He liked Mablethorpe, the small resort on the Lincolnshire coast, and this provides the setting for *Break, break, break*, one of his earliest responses to Hallam's death:

> *Break, break, break,*
> *On thy cold gray stones, O Sea!*
> *And I would that my tongue could utter*
> *The thoughts that arise in me.*

In later years, he experimented with the Lincolnshire dialect. (A Lincolnshire accent was always discernible in his speech.) The best known among these poems is a pair entitled *Northern Farmer: Old Style* and *Northern Farmer: New Style*, written in 1864-65. The old-style farmer, is on his death bed:

> *Doctors, they knawd nout, fur a says what's nawways true;*
> *Naw soort o kind o' use to saay the things that a do.*
> *I've 'ed my point o' aale ivry noight sin' I bean 'ere.*
> *An' I've 'ed my quart ivry market-noight for foorty year.*

The new-style farmer is giving some advice to his son, who is contemplating marriage:

> *Me an' thy muther, Sammy, 'as been a'talking' o' thee;*
> *Thou's bean talkin' to muther, an' she bean telling' it me.*
> *Thou'll not marry for munny – thou's sweet upo' parson's lass –*
> *Noa – thou'll marry for luvv – an' we boath of us think tha an ass.*

Despite the fact that Tennyson never forgot his roots, visitors to Lincolnshire are disappointed to find that Somersby Rectory has not been developed into a museum, in the same way that Dove Cottage in Grasmere has been given over to promoting Wordsworth's life and legacy. Although the church contains a bust of Tennyson, anyone seeking something more substantial must visit Lincoln to see the imposing statue on the east side of the Cathedral.

'The White Hart', Tetford, Tennyson's 'local'. A heavy drinker and a slave to tobacco, Tennyson nevertheless lived to be 83

Fittingly, the Tennyson Research Centre within Lincoln's Central Library is purported to house the most significant collection of his books and manuscripts in the world.

Other places with Tennyson connections including the Vine Hotel in Skegness, the grounds of which are said to have inspired *Come Into The Garden Maud*, and Gunby Hall, which the poet had in mind when he wrote the following lines from *The Palace of Art*:

> *And one, an English home, gray twilight pour'd*
> *On dewy pastures, dewy trees,*
> *Softer than sleep – all things in order stored,*
> *A haunt of ancient peace.*

Jean Ingelow

When Alfred Lord Tennyson died in 1892, it was proposed in America that Jean Ingelow be named as the next Poet Laureate – such was her reputation across the ocean.

Jean Ingelow was born in 1820, Boston, which she described as 'a quiet country town'. Her grandfather was a wealthy banker and ship owner.

His son, Jean's father, was in business with him and they lived off South Street, in adjoining houses overlooking the River Witham. Jean remembered the back of her father's house as being on a level with the wharves. Her nursery was 'a low room in the roof, having a large bow window' with a seat where she spent many a happy hour watching the gangs of men who, at high tide, towed vessels up the river. She also enjoyed watching the 'joyous urchins' playing in the mud, 'picking up empty shells and bits of drift-wood'.

Jean's privileged upbringing came under threat when the family fortunes took a turn for the worse, culminating in the collapse of the business. They moved to Ipswich, where they lived in 'a fine old stone house, with the bank buildings attached … and a large walled garden at the back.' They continued their involvement in banking, until this venture, too, failed. The family ultimately moved to London, where Jean Ingelow spent the rest of her life.

She had been writing poetry since childhood, notably on the shutters of the nursery in Boston. Although some of her work appeared in minor periodicals, she wrote mainly for her own pleasure. A volume of verse, *A Rhyming Chronicle of Incidents and Feelings,* was published in 1850, but it was not until 1863 when *Poems* was published that she became famous.

Her best known poem is *The High Tide on the Coast of Lincolnshire (1571),* of which the following is the first stanza:

The old mayor climb'd the belfry tower,
The ringers ran by two, by three;
"Pull, if ye never pull'd before;
Good ringers, pull your best,: quoth he.
"Play uppe, play uppe, O Boston bells!
Ply all your changes, all your swells,
Play Uppe, 'The Brides of Enderby.'"

She was at her best when writing about the world around her. Although she chose not to mix in fashionable literary circles,

she had many celebrated friends including Tennyson, Christina Rossetti, John Ruskin and Robert Browning, with whom her name was once romantically linked. All expressed their admiration of her poetry, although critics were not always so complimentary when it came to reviewing the prose to which she devoted her later years, describing it as lacking in 'originality and grace' and deploring what they saw as 'weak characterization'.

Contrary to popular belief, the peal of bells, 'The Brides of Enderby', referred to in The High Tide on the Coast of Lincolnshire, was pure fiction, and was never rung as a warning by St. Botolph's in Boston

She lived for many years in Kensington, and it was here, in her house in Holland Street, that she gave her well-known 'copyright dinners'. These were twice-weekly affairs – roast beef one day and boiled mutton the next – laid on for twelve convalescents (poor people recently discharged from local hospitals) chosen by the Kensington clergy. She would also invite groups of factory girls to take tea with her in her garden during the summer months. Patronising these activities may have been, but they were also well-intentioned, proving a welcome treat for the recipients of her charity.

She never married, despite having had a number of admirers in her youth. She shared her Kensington home with her elder brother, William and when he died, in 1886, she continued living there alone. She also stopped writing, although by this time, her popularity had begun to wane.

Jean Ingelow's poetry has not been 'rediscovered' to the degree that one might perhaps have expected. She was a very private person, and her conservative views in relation to the role of women in society have not endeared her to feminists. She had no time for the embryonic women's rights movement, once famously refusing to sign a petition for extending the franchise to women. Instead, she preferred to extol the virtues of domesticity. All women, she said, should pride themselves upon their ability to perform household duties such as cooking and cleaning. Even ironing, she felt, could be developed into a 'graceful and pretty' occupation. In short, she was eminently Victorian – and proud of it.

Foxe's Book of Martyrs

As far as religion was concerned, the Tudor era was particularly bewildering. Under Henry VII, Roman Catholicism was the official religion. The Pope was head of the church, the Bible existed only in Latin editions and monasteries were plentiful. During the reign of Henry VIII, the king became head of the English Church, English versions of the Bible appeared and the monasteries were done away with. When Mary became queen, the country reverted to Catholicism (with a vengeance), only to become Protestant when Elizabeth succeeded to the throne.

John Foxe, whose name came to be reviled in Catholic circles, was born in Boston in 1517. It is known that he entered Brasenose College, Oxford, where he took his B.D. degree in 1538. Five years later, he gained an M.A. at Magdalen College and was elected a Fellow. In 1545, after converting to Protestantism, he was compelled to leave Oxford and, for some years, was reduced to making a living as a tutor in various private households. During the short reign of Edward VI, when Protestants were given rather more latitude, Foxe was ordained as a deacon and published several Protestant tracts. In 1553, upon the accession of Mary, Foxe fled to Germany, thereby avoiding the fate of 280 of his fellow Protestants who were burned at the stake for their beliefs.

In 1552, Foxe had started collecting material for a chronicle of the persecutions suffered by Christians since 1000AD. During his years on the continent, he developed the project and, in 1559, published his findings in a Latin edition of a book entitled *Acts and Monuments,* concentrating (necessarily, one might argue) on atrocities committed by the 'Roman Prelates'.

When he returned home after Mary's death, Foxe became prebend of Salisbury Cathedral and, in 1563, published the first English edition of *Acts and Monuments*, which retailed at an eye-watering ten shillings a copy, making it accessible to only a privileged few. It was seized upon as a vicious attack on the Catholic faith, gaining fame and notoriety as *Foxe's Book of Martyrs*. Foxe argued that the book was more in the way of a history of persecution of the Christian church in general, pointing out that it covered persecutions of Christians by people such as the Emperor Nero and the Persians. Nevertheless, it was the section on the persecutions of Queen Mary's reign which, rightly or wrongly, was recognised as the centrepiece of the work. And it made for gruesome reading. For example, under Mary's rule, John Hooper, Bishop of Worcester and Gloucester, was removed from office and burned at the stake on 9th February 1555. Foxe observes that Hooper was 'three quarters of an hour or more in the fire'. The wind was blowing in the wrong direction so that, initially, Hooper was 'little more than touched'. A second fire was lit, but burned him only 'on the nether parts'. A third fire, 'more extreme than the other two' finished the job, with Hooper beating his breast 'until one of his arms fell off'.

Despite – or, perhaps owing to – the graphic detail of Foxe's accounts, the book was an immediate success and came to symbolise the English Reformation. It was considered sufficiently important to be placed alongside The Bible in cathedral churches. Although

'The Stump and Candle' public house in Boston's Market Place. A blue plaque notes that John Foxe was born in a house which previously occupied the site

sales soared, Foxe did not profit because royalty payments did not exist. Nevertheless, he published three additional, revised editions before his death in 1587.

For the remainder of the sixteenth century, throughout the seventeenth century and into the nineteenth, further editions appeared regularly. As time went on, additional chapters were added, to include the Gunpowder Plot of 1605, the persecution of the Quakers and persecution of French Protestants in the years 1814-20.

Oliver Cromwell was particularly captivated by the book, and it became required reading for his 'Ironsides'. Of course, there were many critics among those who remained faithful to the Catholic religion. The Jesuit priest, Robert Persons, a contemporary of Foxe, described the book as a 'huge dunghill'. To be fair, however, Foxe did not relish the idea of anyone being burnt at the stake, whatever their religion. In 1575, for example, a party of Dutch refugee Anabaptists were arrested in England. Most were deported, but several were imprisoned and two, Hendrik Terwoort and Jan Pieters, went to the stake. Foxe wrote to Elizabeth in an unsuccessful attempt to obtain clemency for them. When this failed, he tried to persuade them to admit the errors of their ways. As far as he was concerned, there was only one true religion.

Controversy surrounding the *Book of Martyrs* continues to this day. Was it an historical work, depicting actual events without prejudice, or was it merely a narrow-minded religious tract?

Foxe himself is remembered in his home town of Boston by a blue plaque mounted on the wall of the 'Stump and Candle' public house in the market place, where stood the house in which he was born.

Chapter Fourteen

ROGUES

The Macaroni Parson

The Church of St Peter & St Paul in Bourne is all that remains of Bourne Abbey, an Augustinian house demolished after 1536 as part of the Dissolution of the Monasteries. In 1729, the wife of the rector, the Reverend William Dodd, presented him with a son, who would also be christened William.

The Reverend Dodd was poor in that he had no source of income save that from his living. The only chance William had of attending university was to sit for a sizarship. This was a scheme run by the University of Cambridge (and Trinity College, Dublin) whereby students received an allowance from their college to enable them to study. In return, the student would perform certain domestic duties, such as waiting upon his fellow students at meal times.

William attained his sizarship and entered Clare Hall, Cambridge. To help support himself, he also wrote – successfully – thereby increasing the scanty allowance his father was able to make him. In 1749, despite his disadvantages, he gained a first class degree. He could have sought preferment at Cambridge, but chose, instead, to seek his fortune in London. He continued to write, in both verse and prose, and gained something of a reputation for his wit as a conversationalist and public speaker.

The capital also held appeal for Dodd in terms of the opportunities it provided for meeting women. Dodd had certainly worked hard during his undergraduate days, but he had also played hard, displaying his love for female companionship and also a tendency for living beyond his means. In 1751, he married Mary Perkins, the daughter of a domestic servant, the newlyweds setting up home in Wardour Street, which Dodd furnished to the highest standards.

At his father's insistence, however, Dodd gave up his life in London and took holy orders, taking on the duties of a curate in West Ham. This period saw the production of one of his most celebrated literary works, *The Beauties of Shakespeare*. He moved on to St James in Garlick Hill, where he held a lectureship and then to St. Olave's in Hart Street. In 1758, he became the first chaplain of the newly opened Magdalen House, a home for prostitutes in Great Prescot Street.

The following year, Dodd took his MA, increasing his prestige and his income by assuming the role of tutor to the sons of gentlemen, including young Philip Stanhope, heir to the title and estates of the Earl of Chesterfield. He became chaplain-in-ordinary to George III and, in 1766, received his LL.D from Cambridge.

Dodd had been living in a modest house at West Ham, but shortly after becoming a Doctor of Laws, he exchanged it for a grander home in Southampton Row. Later, he acquired a second home, a country house in Ealing, and travelled between the two residences in a luxurious coach.

For a time, it seemed that his income would keep pace with his expenditure, for he won £1,000 in a lottery. He used it to build his own proprietary chapel (i.e. with seats going to private subscribers) in Pimlico and bought shares in another in Bloomsbury. He also secured two livings, in Hockliffe and Chalgrove. To top it all, in 1773 the Earl of Chesterfield died, and young Philip Stanhope succeeded. The new earl promptly made Dodd his chaplain. Then, just as all seemed to be set fair, Dodd set in motion a series of events which were to lead him to the gallows.

Lady Apsley, wife of the Lord Chancellor, received an anonymous latter offering her the sum of £3,000 if she could secure, for a person to be named later, the then vacant living of the richly endowed parish of St. George's in Hanover Square, the patronage of which was her husband's. The letter was traced back to Dodd. When George III heard of it, he dismissed Dodd from his office as chaplain. The scurrilous news-sheets of the eighteenth century held him up to public ridicule, and he fled abroad.

He returned to England in 1776, when the loyal Lord Chesterfield offered him the living of Wing, in Buckinghamshire. And yet, once back in England, he resumed his extravagant lifestyle. He had already sacrificed much goodwill by openly consorting with Polly Kennedy, 'a noted woman of the town', and he was now seen in dubious company at a race meeting – his foppish dress leading to the press lampooning him as 'The Macaroni Parson'.

Sorely pressed by his creditors, he was forced to sell his chapel and, in an act of sheer desperation, he forged the signature of Lord Chesterfield on a bond for £4,200, subsequently receiving a banker's loan on the strength of it. When the fraud was discovered, as it was bound to be, Dodd was arrested and put on trial for what was then the capital offence of forgery. His defence that he was culpable only of arranging an irregular loan, was rejected. He was found guilty and sentenced to death. A recommendation for mercy was rejected by the king.

However, Dodd still had many friends, and a petition for clemency attracted 30,000 signatures. His cause also won the support of Dr. Samuel Johnson, who famously composed a sermon 'The Convict's Address to his unhappy Brethren', delivered in the chapel of Newgate prison. Johnson never went to see Dodd, but he had already assisted him by writing a statement for him to make prior to the pronouncement of sentence and later wrote an impassioned letter (for Dodd's signature) to the king.

Notwithstanding the great man's efforts, Dodd was hanged at Tyburn on 27th June 1777. As Johnson generously recorded, Dodd 'was at first what he endeavoured to make others; but the world broke down his resolution, and he in time ceased to exemplify his own instructions'.

'The First Highwayman'

The Oxford English Dictionary notes that the word 'highwayman' was first used in 1649, and relates to one who frequents the highway for the purpose of robbing passengers – especially one who is mounted as distinct from going on foot.

The highwayman was essentially a seventeenth to early nineteenth century phenomenon. His targets were often passenger and mail coaches as well as individual travellers. Oddly, he developed into something of a romantic figure, in the guise of characters such as James Hind, Claude Duval and Dick Turpin.

Turpin, going under the name of John Palmer, spent several months residing at Long Sutton in Lincolnshire, where he was accused of sheep stealing and horse theft. One of the earliest – if not the earliest – highwaymen was a Lincolnshire man born and bred. He operated in the early seventeenth century, and he was called Gamaliel Ratsey.

Ratsey was born, probably around 1580, in Market Deeping. It is known that he came from a respected family and that he received a sound education. In 1599, he enlisted as a soldier in the army of the Earl of Essex that was sent to Ireland to quell the Earl of Tyrone's rebellion. He remained in Ireland throughout hostilities, earning the 'commendations of his Commanders' and a promotion to sergeant. When the campaign ended, in 1603, Ratsey was demobilised and returned to England.

He lost no time in putting together a gang and embarking upon a career of highway robbery. His cohorts probably included ex-soldiers like himself. Chief among them were two individuals named George Snell and Henry Shorthose. The pair are named in two pamphlets published in 1605, after Ratsey's death, and which constitute the sole source of reference for his exploits. The incidents outlined in these pamphlets – both best-sellers – set the standard for the public's expectations of a highwayman.

Ideally, a highwayman should be a 'gentleman'. In this respect, Ratsey's background was a respectable one and, if his recorded exploits are to be believed, he often demonstrated a familiarity with learning. On one occasion, prior to robbing 'a Scholler of Cambridge', he rode with him for some way, talking to him 'of many matters', thoroughly convincing his prey that he presented no threat to him. And, when meeting a company of actors at an inn, he persuaded them to perform 'a private play before him', afterwards dispensing advice to the head of the company on how best to conduct his business.

Nothing amused common folk more than instances of a highwayman tweaking the nose of authority – particularly the law. When Lincolnshire (where he committed many of his crimes) grew too hot to hold him, he led his gang into Norfolk. Travelling by night in foul weather, they lost their way. When they were within three or four miles of Wisbech, Ratsey had the gall to knock up the household of a Justice of the Peace to request a guide to take them into the town. The JP's wife graciously instructed one of her servants to perform the task.

Again, when robbing a lawyer in Lambeth, Ratsey berated the man sharply, informing him that he had no pity for vultures who would 'picke every poore mannes pocket ... till you leave them never a penny to bless themselves'. Ratsey also pointed out to the lawyer that if he robbed a poor man and recognised him as 'indigent and needy', it was his practice to return his purse with a little extra to help him along.

The principle of taking from the rich and giving to the poor is an essential part of the highwayman's baggage. An example is to be found in Ratsey's treatment of an elderly couple he met going to a fair in St. Ives, between Huntingdon and Cambridge. When informed that Ratsey must have their money, the old man assured him that 'in all world he had but five nobles'. Although Ratsey went ahead with the robbery, he listened to the couple's woes and ended up returning the cash, together with forty shillings of his own.

A highwayman must also demonstrate chivalrous behaviour towards women. One day, Ratsey encountered the daughter of a parson 'dwelling near Stamford', initially relieving her of forty shillings with which she intended to buy 'stuff to make her a gown'. When she pleaded that it would be years before her father gave her any more money for a dress, Ratsey returned her purse and, putting his hand in his pocket, gave her another thirty shillings, 'bidding her to buy her a petticoat also'.

Perhaps it goes without saying that a highwayman must be fearless. In Northamptonshire, he single-handedly robbed nine travellers. They were all Lincolnshire men and Ratsey was recognised by one of them, who knew him to be 'a dangerous and desperate fellow'. As was customary in such matters, they pleaded poverty, but Ratsey would not be discouraged and, after being threatened with the loss of life and limb, they handed over two hundred pounds.

Such is the aura of invincibility surrounding the highwayman, that it would be unthinkable for him to meet his doom by being outwitted by the law. And so, Ratsey is, at length, betrayed by his unworthy companions, Snell and Shorthose. The three robbed a 'Gentleman and his brother' near Bedford. The victims put up a fight and although Ratsey was hurt 'very dangerously', the three escaped to Saffron Walden, where they laid low for a time. Afterwards making their way to London, they divided the loot at an inn in Southwark. Ratsey took a double share 'in respect of his hurts received', which may have been resented by his colleagues.

In any event, Snell was shortly apprehended in Duck Lane for a robbery he had committed alone. In exchange for a promise of leniency, he betrayed Ratsey, who was taken near Doctors Commons and committed to Newgate, where he was joined, a few weeks later, by Shorthose, who was arrested in Long Lane. All three were tried at the Spring Assizes, where they were found guilty of the Bedfordshire robbery and condemned to death. Ratsey was hanged at Tyburn on 26th March 1605.

His career as a highwayman had lasted less than two years, but in that time, he had become a household name. In *The Alchemist*, first performed in 1610, Ben Jonson could write of a 'face cut … worse than Gamaliel Ratsey's', knowing that his audience would have no difficulty making the connection. (Jonson was referring not to Ratsey's visage, but to the gruesome mask he habitually wore when carrying out his robberies.)

During his time in Newgate, Ratsey penned a rambling poem comprising 41 verses, entitled *Ratsey's Repentance*, in which he abjures others to learn by his example:

Villains avaunt, you bastards are by kinde,
That doe perturbe the Countries quiet state,
Shame to offend, shun a corrupted mind,
And learne by me your former life to hate.

Robert Augustus Delaney

Robert Augustus ('Gussie') Delaney liked to see himself as a gentleman jewel thief – a sort of 'Raffles', E. W. Hornung's fictional gentleman cracksman; a likeable, debonair rogue, always willing to help a chap down on his luck. Delaney was none of these things. There was one other notable difference: Raffles didn't get caught, whereas Delaney spent twenty years of his life incarcerated in various prisons.

Raised in South Africa, Delaney came to England during the First World War. In 1915, at the age of 24, he married a wealthy Lincolnshire widow twelve years his senior and posed as a 'gentleman' farmer, buying a fine house, 'The Limes', at Swineshead, near Boston. In 1922, having spent all his wife's money, he ran off with her niece. For a few months, the pair ran a boarding house in Westcliffe-on-Sea, Essex. They parted company after the premises were severely damaged by a fire – probably started by Delaney, who subsequently made an outrageous insurance claim.

After this, he moved on to London, where he began his career as a cat-burglar. Clad in evening dress, he would shin up drainpipes to gain entry to the houses of the rich and titled in the capital's West End. His spree, during which he stole £30,000 worth of jewellery, was brought to an end by a young detective called Robert Fabian who traced him to a flat in Half Moon Street.

It was Fabian, as the celebrated 'Fabian Of the Yard', who would do much to cement Delaney's reputation as the very first cat-burglar, marvelling at the acrobatic prowess he displayed in the execution of his crimes. Of course, Fabian must have known that the term 'cat-burglar' had been in use for many years. Similarly, he would have been aware of the most infamous cat-burglar of them all, Charlie Peace who, half a century earlier – and despite walking with a limp and having a maimed left hand – displayed all the agility of Delaney in the execution of his crimes.

Ultimately convicted of a total of six Park Lane burglaries, Delaney went to gaol for three years. Upon his release in 1927, he paid a return visit to Swineshead. In the early hours of 29 October, he and a confederate, John Brown, broke into the garage of his old home, 'The Limes' and stole an Austin car belonging to Charles Collins, to whom Delaney had sold the house and who still lived there. Then they drove to the farm offices of William Gilding Ltd, also known to Delaney, which they proceeded to burgle.

Still using the stolen Austin, Delaney and Brown made their way onto the A15, which would take them to Peterborough and on to London. Their luck turned on the notorious horseshoe bend at Aswarby, where they spun off the road into a ditch. Their presence was reported to the police by a passing motorist. When officers arrived, Delaney tried to pass himself off as Collins, explaining that he was on his way to Peterborough on business. Unfortunately, a shotgun (part of the proceeds of the robbery) lay on the back seat of the car, and it was thought expedient to take the duo into Sleaford for further questioning. En route, they made a desperate bid for freedom, in the course of which Delaney drew a revolver. After a struggle, they were overpowered and held at Sleaford Police Station. Boston Magistrates' Court committed them for trial at Derbyshire Assizes, where Delaney claimed, unconvincingly, that he had found Collins' car in the ditch and had intended returning it to him. Brown was sentenced to three years imprisonment while Delaney, as senior partner in the enterprise, got seven years.

Released from gaol in October 1933, he was soon back at work. Now in his forties, he had lost some of his agility and, having suffered one or two bad falls during his nocturnal excursions, he engaged an apprentice – a 16-year-old youth who was prepared to undertake much of the legwork, in exchange for learning the trade. It was during this brief period of freedom that Delaney wrote his life story in a series of articles for *Thomson's Weekly News*. This could only draw attention to his activities, but perhaps it didn't matter, for the police were already watching him.

The treacherous bend at Aswarby on the A15, where Augustus Delaney came to grief in a stolen car in the early hours of 29th October 1927

In November 1934, he was arrested and charged with committing burglaries in London and Bexhill-on-Sea. This time, he was sentenced to nine years' imprisonment. Released on licence in 1940, he was back inside the following year. June 1945 saw him returned to the streets, but by the end of the year, he was appearing at Sussex Assizes in Lewes, charged with two counts of burglary. His sentence of four years imprisonment would be his last, for in 1948 he died of a heart attack while serving out his time in HMP Parkhurst.

Like many petty crooks, Delaney held himself in high esteem, boasting about his impressive hauls of jewellery. While the face value of the items he stole might run into thousands of pounds, however, he would receive only a fraction of their true worth from fences. Apart from the Swineshead years, when he lived the high life on his wife's money, his was a precarious, itinerant, hand-to-mouth existence. As far as Robert Augustus Delaney was concerned, crime most definitely did not pay.

Chapter Fifteen

POLITICAL LINCOLNSHIRE

The Lincolnshire Rising of 1536

'the rude commons of one shire, and that the most brute and beastly in the whole realm'

– so said King Henry VIII of the people of Lincolnshire upon the occasion of a county-wide demonstration against his religious and financial policies. Whether they were the 'most brute and beastly' in his kingdom is a moot point, but he was wrong in his assessment of the discontent as being limited to a single shire, for it soon spread into Yorkshire, to culminate in The Pilgrimage of Grace.

At the heart of the matter was the 'Dissolution of the Monasteries'. In addition to their spiritual function as houses of prayer, the monasteries offered a range of more 'practical' services. Hospitality was given to travellers, alms and food were distributed to the poor, medical care was often provided and they were recognised as centres of learning – especially for their production of illuminated manuscripts. The monasteries were also major landowners, with a total of around 6% of the nation's arable land rented out to tenant farmers.

Unfortunately, by the early sixteenth century, many monasteries, having failed to keep up with the times, were poorly managed. The king, moreover, was extravagant, and by seizing the monasteries' not inconsiderable assets, he hoped to tackle his ongoing debt problem. Therefore, in 1536, his government passed the Act of Suppression through which around 400 of the smaller monasteries were closed and their assets seized. One of the 'victims' was Louth Park Abbey in Lincolnshire. Established in the twelfth century, it had been in decline for many years and, by the time of its closure on 8th September 1536, only the abbot and ten monks remained in residence. It was in Louth that the Lincolnshire Rising against Henry's policy began.

On Sunday 1st October 1536, the Reverend Thomas Kendall delivered an 'emotive sermon' in St. James's Church in Louth. It was feared that churches, like the monasteries, would be stripped of their treasures, and the King's Commissioners were due to arrive to assess the wealth of St. James's, which was said to be considerable. As a result, some members of the congregation took

the keys to the church, which were given to a shoemaker, Nicholas Melton. Under the name of 'Captain Cobbler', he became the leader of the Louth protestors. The next morning, they rang the church bells to raise the townsfolk to action.

Trouble was also brewing in other towns,

Commemorative plaque outside St. James's Church, Louth, birthplace of The Lincolnshire Rising particularly in Horncastle, where the church bells were also rung. One of the ringleaders was William Leech, a sheep farmer from Fulletby. On 3rd October, he organised a march to Scrivelsby to confront Sir Edward Dymoke. As the Sheriff of Lincolnshire, it was Dymoke's job to deal with insurrection but he caved in to threats and agreed to join the rising.

The following day, the mob, brandishing the Dymoke family banner, moved on to Old Bolingbroke to confront Dr. John Raynes, the Bishop of Lincoln's Chancellor. Apparently, he was ill in bed, but it may be that he was only feigning sickness in

This gaunt crag is all that remains of Kirkstead Abbey. The last abbot, Richard Harrison, was executed for his participation in the Lincolnshire Rising

an attempt to elicit sympathy. Whatever the case, he was put on a horse and conveyed to Horncastle where he was set upon and beaten to death. Another casualty was one of Thomas Cromwell's men, Thomas Wolsey (possibly a relation of the late Cardinal Wolsey), who was lynched.

On Thursday 5th October, the host began to make its way to Lincoln. En route, the monks of the religious houses at Kirkstead Abbey and Barlings Abbey were pressed into service. At Barlings, the abbot, Matthew Mackerell, put up some initial resistance, but the mob broke into the Abbey, commandeered provisions and spent the night in the barns and offices. Friday saw the protestors' ranks swelled by men from other localities, including Louth and Caistor, as they approached Lincoln. Although contemporary estimates of the numbers involved are as high as 50,000, it is likely that a maximum of 20,000 is nearer the mark. Again, while it is implied that a march was made on Lincoln Cathedral, the vast majority probably camped out, although the gentry may have been accommodated in the city.

Although the protestors lacked a long-term strategy, it was decided to send a list of their concerns to the king. These included the Dissolution of the Monasteries, the imposition of new taxes and the appointment and promotion of Thomas Cromwell and others 'of low birth and small reputation' to positions of authority.

On 11th October, Henry's reply arrived. Justifying the suppression of the monasteries, he took his subjects to task for having the temerity to question his authority, ordering the protestors to disband, deliver up the ringleaders and submit themselves to whatever punishment might be deemed appropriate.

This was enough for the majority who meekly returned to their homes as directed, despite the admonitions of the ringleaders, who knew that they themselves could expect little mercy.

With the arrival of an armed force led by the Duke of Suffolk, the process of retribution began. On 22nd October, two hundred men of Louth took an oath of loyalty to the king and gave up fifteen of the ringleaders. The process continued for several months as more participants were identified, arrested, interrogated and, in a number of cases, executed.

Some were lucky. Sir Edward Dymoke, for example, successfully claimed that he had been coerced into joining the insurrection. However, the abbots of Kirkstead and Barlings, along with several monks, did not escape the ultimate penalty – the authorities eagerly grasping at the opportunity to accelerate the process of dissolution. The king had demanded one hundred heads but, although roughly that number of insurgents were brought to trial, only about a third were condemned to death. Some who would have stood trial died during their imprisonment at Lincoln Castle. Among the latter was probably 'Captain Cobbler', of whose trial and execution there is no record.

A few insurgents may have decided to move on, to join the developing and more peaceful Yorkshire rising known as The Pilgrimage of Grace. Lord John Hussey of Sleaford, who had arguably been active in suppressing the Lincolnshire Rising supported the Yorkshire insurrection, and paid for his error of judgement with his life.

It all amounts to a sorry episode in the history of Lincolnshire, reflecting badly upon those who chose to rebel, and also upon the king, whose response might have been more conciliatory.

William Cecil, Lord Burghley

William Cecil, undoubtedly one of England's greatest statesmen, was born in 1620 in Bourne. He received his early education at The King's School, Grantham and Stamford School before going up to St. John's, Cambridge.

Elected as MP for Stamford in 1547, he was given a minor role in the Duke of Somerset's protectorate, empowered to govern during the minority of Edward VI. When Somerset was ousted, Cecil was confined to the Tower of London for three months.

Burghley House, built by William Cecil, Lord Burghley. (Author's collection)

After making friends with Somerset's successor, the Duke of Northumberland, he signed up to the Duke's plan to bar the daughters of Henry VIII, Mary and Elizabeth, from the succession, in favour of Lady Jane Grey. He had tried, unsuccessfully, to get out of doing so by feigning sickness, but he did manage to cover his back by secretly opposing the scheme, and when Mary did become queen, he was able to argue that he had supported her all along. The ability to deceive one's enemies was the first essential of statecraft in those perilous times, and Cecil had already established his credentials as a master of the technique.

He was also involved in the management of Princess Elizabeth's estates and, in this capacity, he was able to work his way into the future queen's good graces. When Elizabeth succeeded to the throne in 1558, his future was set fair, for Elizabeth was already accustomed to depending upon his judgement.

For forty years, Elizabeth and Cecil worked together for the good of the country. His advice was not always heeded, but he knew when it was wise to let go of concepts with which Elizabeth had little sympathy. He also knew how important he was to her. She knew it too, and encouraged him in this belief. His advancement proceeded smoothly from the office of Secretary of State, to Lord High Treasurer and Lord Privy Seal. In 1571, he was given the title Baron Burghley.

Although the relationship had a firm foundation, it was not without its rocky moments – notably in the long-running saga of Mary, Queen of Scots. In his dealings with Mary – a prisoner in England from 1572 – he showed sympathy in his desire to comply with Elizabeth's plans to reach an understanding with her sister, but he also believed that, sooner or later (preferably the former) Mary must die. He advised Elizabeth against recognising Mary's claim to the throne of Scotland, arguing that she would always pose a threat to her security. Notwithstanding his views, Cecil was put in charge of negotiations with Mary. It is a credit to his fair-mindedness that he came away thinking that it might be possible to reach an agreement to suit all parties. Then, he uncovered the Ridolfi Plot of 1572, involving the Duke of Norfolk, designed to depose Elizabeth in favour of Mary.

Norfolk was condemned to death, but Elizabeth baulked at signing the order for his execution, prompting Cecil to observe that by her innate propensity to be merciful, she 'hath taken more harm than by justice'. When Cecil put the full details of the plot before her, however, she knew she had no alternative.

Mary remained in captivity until 1587, when her alleged involvement in the Babington Plot to supplant Elizabeth finally led to her trial and execution. Once again, the queen prevaricated over putting her signature on the death warrant, but the Council remained firm. Mary was executed and Cecil found himself on the receiving end of one of Elizabeth's intimidating temper tantrums. He was quite prepared to bear the brunt her rage. That was one of his functions.

Cecil's greatest challenges, however, came in the guise of the queen's favourites. The first of these was Robert Dudley, whom Elizabeth created Earl of Leicester. She also appointed him to the Privy Council, where he became part of a conspiracy to oust Cecil. Leicester decided it would be in his best interests to inform the queen of the plot and it fizzled out. So did his dalliance with Elizabeth when he married another, although he retained some influence with her until his death in 1588.

Robert Devereux, Earl of Essex, more than 30 years younger than Elizabeth, was more mercurial than Dudley. He, too, was appointed to the Privy Council, where he and Cecil constantly clashed. When Cecil died, in 1598, Elizabeth appointed his son, Robert as his successor to the post of Lord Privy Seal. Essex was furious, his discontent eventually leading him into open rebellion and, ultimately, the executioner's axe.

Although good government was high on William Cecil's list of priorities, he did have one thing in common with both Dudley and Devereux: all were keen to profit by the influential positions which they occupied. Funds to increase the salaries of government ministers were always in short supply, and so it was customary for anyone who had the queen's ear to levy charges from those who wished to procure favour. At one point, Cecil was receiving a hundred letters a day from people who wanted him to further their interests at court. Dudley and Essex were his greatest rivals in the business of extorting lobbying fees but, unlike either of them, he was shrewd enough to plead poverty when challenged. In 1553, he inherited Burghley House from his father, and immediately set about transforming it into a palace. Such was his personal wealth that he was able to build a second one – Theobalds in Hertfordshire – from scratch.

Cecil's achievement in retaining his position for so many years in an environment where treachery and duplicity were part and parcel of daily life is remarkable, and he well deserves the epitaph of 'the greatest counsellor in Christendom.'

The Iron Lady

The Grantham of the 1920s, birthplace of Britain's first woman Prime Minister, was very different to the Grantham of today. With a population of 20,000, it was a centre for agricultural engineering. There was a bustling Saturday market, the Great North Road ran through the town and you could still see daylight between Grantham and the villages of Great Gonerby and Manthorpe. On the corner of North Parade and Brook Street stood a grocer's shop, owned by Alfred Roberts. This is where his daughter Margaret was born, on 13th October 1925.

The family lived above the shop and the business was a way of life. Everyone took a turn serving in the shop and it was only possible to take a holiday of one week each year. In those days, shopkeepers would pore over their ledgers into the early hours, conscientiously searching for discrepancies of a few pennies. Above all, one paid one's way in the world. A business which borrowed money was a sure sign of a business in trouble. Alf Robert's neighbours would have looked up to him because he ran his own business, little knowing what it cost the family in terms of commitment and sheer hard work. This was the world in which Margaret Thatcher grew up. Its values and principles remained with her for life.

She was educated at Grantham Girls' School, from where she progressed to Somerville College, Oxford, where she studied chemistry. Her first serious foray into politics took place in 1950, when she stood, unsuccessfully, as the Conservative candidate for Dartford, a safe Labour seat. Later, she married and began practising law, which she had studied in her spare time. She also married and gave birth to a son and daughter. Returning to politics at the General Election of 1959, she was elected MP for the north London seat of Finchley and was given a junior ministerial post at the Ministry of Pensions.

In Edward Heath's government of 1970-74 she became Minister for Education, receiving a lot of bad publicity when she

The corner shop in Grantham where Margaret Thatcher spent her childhood

introduced a law banning free school milk and another increasing the price of school dinners. When the Conservatives lost the next General Election, Margaret replaced Edward Heath as party leader. In 1979, the Conservatives were returned to power, and Margaret Thatcher became Prime Minister – an office she retained until 1990.

Throughout her career, Thatcher's qualities of resolve and tenacity often served her well, as in the Falklands War of 1982. Following the British victory over Argentina, it was suggested by the American President, Ronald Reagan, that the question of the Islands' sovereignty should be decided by the United Nations. His suggestion was peremptorily dismissed. She also triumphed in her battle with the National Union of Miners, who brought their members out on strike for a year in 1984-85, although the nation was divided in its response to her actions. While many people resented the power wielded by the more militant of the trade unions, such as the NUM, the programme of pit closures led to the destruction of entire communities.

Many of her domestic policies fell into this 'divisive' category. Her government raised an enormous sum from the sale of council houses. While the occupants who were able to buy them at knockdown prices were able to aspire to home ownership, the policy led to an acute shortage of council properties. Similarly, privatisation of nationalised industries led, on the one hand, to greater efficiency and profitability but, on the other, to increased unemployment and higher prices. Her old mentor, Harold MacMillan, likened it to selling off the family silver.

Her most unpopular policy and one which contributed heavily to her downfall was the attempt to introduce a new Community Charge or 'poll tax' as it came to be known. The intention was to replace the local government tax – 'the rates', based on the value of a house – with a levy on all adult occupants of a house, regardless of its value. The unpopularity of the measure led to riots and many people simply refused to pay it – so many, in fact, that it became unenforceable.

The problem with tenacity is that it can very easily develop into stubbornness, and this happened with Margaret Thatcher. The decline in her popularity merely increased her determination to cling to her position, turning what could have been a dignified resignation into a bitter, doomed fight for survival.

Her major domestic achievement lay in the great strides she made towards balancing the books, cutting the National Debt from 43% of GDP to 26%. The country, she thought, just like the shopkeepers of her youth, must live within its means. Unfortunately, this philosophy was outdated, for the era of unlimited credit had arrived. On both a personal and a national level, money to spend today could be borrowed. Tomorrow would take care of itself.

Chapter Sixteen

WARRIORS

The Last Englishman

The title of 'The Last Englishman' has been conferred on the outlaw and opponent of Norman oppression, Hereward the Wake. The stories of his exploits are the stuff of legend and befit the persona of a folk hero, making it all the harder to differentiate between fact and fiction.

The generally accepted place of Hereward's birth is Bourne; the date of his birth around 1035. He grew up to be an errant youth, a constant source of trouble to his father, a Danish thegn. At the age of 18, he was outlawed and exiled by the English king, Edward the Confessor. Crossing the sea to Flanders, he became a mercenary in the service of Count Baldwin V.

He was still there in 1066 when the Normans invaded England. A few years later, in 1069, he made a brief return to England. Some sources have him visiting an uncle, Abbot Brand of Peterborough Abbey. According to others, he returned to seek revenge, having received news that the Normans had killed his brother and occupied the family estate. Surprising the culprits while they were indulging themselves at a feast, he killed fifteen of them virtually single-handed, before fleeing back to Flanders.

In 1070, Hereward was back in England, raiding the fen country as the leader of a group of resistance fighters against Norman rule. He was among those who welcomed an army of Danes who planned to set up a temporary base on the Isle of Ely, and he subsequently joined them in sacking Peterborough Abbey. Hereward considered the Abbey fair game because a Norman had been appointed to the abbacy following the recent death of Abbot Brand. However, the Danes soon departed with their booty, leaving Hereward to take the consequences. He decided to make a stand, becoming a focus for the hardcore of the opposition to Norman rule. Among the two or three thousand dissidents who joined him were Edwin and Morcar, the former Saxon earls of Mercia and Northumbria respectively. Both had fought the invading Vikings at the Battle of Fulford in 1066.

In late 1071, King William led an army of one thousand men to deal with them and Hereward was forced into retreating to the Isle of Ely. At that time, the Isle of Ely was, indeed, an island. Surrounded by treacherous marshland, it was home to an abbey, established a century earlier. In addition to a network of peat defences, Hereward had built a wooden fort, but his men also occupied the abbey, eating and sleeping alongside the monks, some of whom also took part in the fighting.

William approached Hereward's stronghold via Cambridge, advancing from there to what is the present-day village of Aldreth. He lost no time in organising the construction of a huge timber causeway across the marshes. This contraption, probably thrown together too hastily, collapsed and many Normans, thrown into the swamp, were drowned.

Following a temporary withdrawal to regroup, the king returned to Aldreth to make a second attempt at building a causeway. While the work was progressing, Hereward, in the guise of a fisherman, is supposed to have mingled with his enemies in an attempt to gain intelligence. He would have noted that the Normans were building wooden towers of their own, from which catapults could operate. Clearly, William was a man who preferred pitched battles; he was not at all comfortable dealing with the guerrilla tactics of a hidden enemy. While the work was progressing, Hereward and his men launched an unexpected assault. One of his most valuable weapons was fire. The causeway and the wooden towers were set alight, the flames quickly spreading to the reed beds. Once again, the Normans retreated in confusion.

In the end, Hereward was beaten by the treachery of Thurstan, Abbot of Ely. Thurstan knew that when William finally triumphed – as he must – the abbey could well be razed to the ground. So, in return for a guarantee of safety, the monks guided the Normans to an easier path through the marshes. William was able to set up his siege engines on reasonably dry land in sight of the peat defences, and this time, instead of a rickety, cumbersome causeway, a bridge of boats was assembled in readiness for a swift advance.

After a bombardment of several days' duration, many of the defenders fled and the Normans, at long last, were able to cross over and pursue them. Casualties among the defenders were high and the king's justice swift and cruel, many of those suspected of being ringleaders having limbs hacked off. Edwin and Morcar, at least in the short term, were taken into the fold, but Hereward escaped. Accounts of his ultimate fate vary enormously. He may have continued his life as an outlaw, or he could have returned to Flanders, there to resume his old life as a mercenary. It seems unlikely that he would have made his peace with William, as some sources suggest, to die at a ripe old age on his restored estates.

It is thanks largely to the Victorian novelist, Charles Kingsley, that Hereward was rescued from obscurity. Kingsley's historical novel, *Hereward the Wake*, published in 1866, proved immensely popular. Appropriately, Kingsley penned the work in the old vicarage attached to St. Michael's & All Angels Church in Edenham, near Bourne.

The Earl of Lindsey

Born in 1583, Robert Bertie was an Elizabethan – indeed, the queen was his godmother. His father, Peregrine Bertie, was 13th Baron Willoughby de Eresby; his mother, Mary de Vere, daughter of the 16th Earl of Oxford.

As a youth, he participated in the Anglo-Spanish War of 1585-1604, acquitting himself well in the successful raid on the Spanish port of Cadiz in 1596. Like many of his contemporaries, he went on to fight in war-torn mainland Europe, serving King Christian IV of Denmark in the Kalmar War against Sweden, and then Prince Maurice of Nassau in the Dutch War of Independence against Spain.

In 1626, he was created Earl of Lindsey, and fought in the Anglo-French War of 1627-29. The English, in support of Protestant Huguenots struggling against Louis XIII of France, mounted a number of expeditions aimed at relieving the Huguenots under siege in La Rochelle. Lindsey joined the Duke of Buckingham in the first such venture, which was a disastrous failure. In 1628, after Buckingham's death, Lindsay was made Admiral of the Fleet, and made a second failed attempt at lifting the siege.

Throughout the 1630s, Lindsey spent much of his time seeking to improve his fenland estates in Lincolnshire through drainage schemes. He must have thought that his military career was over, but during part of the Bishops Wars with Scotland in 1639-40, he served as Governor of Berwick. The Scottish victory edged England closer to civil war. As Lord Lieutenant of Lincolnshire, a post which he had held since 1629, Lindsey should have been in a position to raise the militia on the king's behalf, but Parliament withdrew his commission in February 1642, whereupon he marched with his own privately raised regiment to join King Charles I at York.

Charles officially began his campaign by raising the Royal Standard at Nottingham on 22nd August 1642 and Lindsey was appointed General-in-Chief of the army. It was only a matter of time before a major clash of arms between the king's forces and those of Parliament took place. The inevitable encounter occurred just eight weeks later, at Edgehill in Warwickshire. Some 14,000 Royalists occupied the Edgehill escarpment above the village of Kineton, while the 12,000 strong Parliamentarian army, commanded by Robert Devereux, Earl of Essex, deployed on the plain below.

Tensions within the Royalist leadership had been simmering for weeks. Although Lindsey was supposed to be General-in-Chief, in practice, however, he had no overall authority. Prince Rupert, as Lieutenant-General of Horse, enjoyed control over the cavalry, and reported directly to the king. While Lindsey knew that cavalry and infantry should be used in concert, Rupert liked to act independently – an attitude that would eventually cost the Royalists the war. The arrival of the 70-year-old Earl of Forth and his command lessened Lindsey's sphere of influence still further because, despite the difference in their ages, Forth and Rupert seem to have got on well together. Lindsey became ever more isolated.

Tempers finally boiled over with a disagreement over tactics. Lindsey's preference, given his own experience in the field, was for deployment using the simplistic Dutch model. Rupert, on the other hand, preferred the more elaborate Swedish system. In this, Rupert was supported by the Earl of Forth who, in his younger days, had fought in the Swedish service. It all proved too much for Lindsey. Having to countenance Rupert's independence was bad enough, but the Prince's interference in the deployment of his infantry was intolerable. The General-in-Chief resigned, though not before throwing a tantrum in front of the troops and announcing that he would die fighting at the head of his own regiment. Forth assumed command.

In the early afternoon of 23rd October 1642, the two flanking groups of horse and the central infantry of each army stood firm during a mutual artillery bombardment lasting an hour. Then

Prince Rupert advanced from the Royalist right, shattering the Parliamentarian left wing, before galloping on to Kineton which his men proceeded to plunder. A parallel advance by the Royalist horse on the left was not so successful and a portion of the Parliamentarian cavalry was able to wheel in on the Royalist infantry which was engaged in a dour struggle with its Parliamentarian counterpart. The Royalists were steadily pushed back, being saved from defeat only by the opportune return of Rupert to the battlefield. The fighting began to subside and both sides withdrew as darkness fell. During the night, Essex marched off to Warwick, leaving the king to enjoy a technical victory.

Hollow as it might be, it was not a triumph that Lindsey would be able to enjoy. He had proved as good as his word for, during the battle, he was wounded in the thigh – probably by a musket ball – and carried to what was described as 'a poor house' where he was laid upon some straw. His wound was serious, but it was thought that if he had been attended by surgeons, he might have survived. Some levelled the blame at the Earl of Essex for the failure to procure medical aid, claiming that he harboured a grudge against Lindsey. However, the Civil War chronicler, the Earl of Clarendon, states that 'about midnight, he [Essex] sent Sir William Balfour and some other officer to see him, and to offer him all offices, and meant himself to have visited him.'

Lindsey's visitors found him in a bullish mood. Upbraiding them for their engagement in 'so foul a rebellion', he accused Balfour of 'the most odious ingratitude' towards the king. Essex, he added, 'ought to cast himself at the king's feet to beg his pardon.' So vociferous did he become, that the officers withdrew and prevented Essex from making a personal visit. Although surgeons *were* sent, Lindsey had lost too much blood and died before morning. His passing, says Clarendon, was considered to be a great loss 'to all who knew him.'

Gonville Bromhead VC

Lincolnshire has three small settlements called Thurlby, one of which lies eight miles to the west of Lincoln, off the A46. Here is located Thurlby Hall, one-time seat of the Bromhead family.

The Bromheads boasted a fine military pedigree. Colonel John Bromhead fought in the Napoleonic Wars, while Lieutenant-General Sir Gonville Bromhead saw action in the American War of Independence. The most celebrated of all was Lieutenant Gonville Bromhead, who was awarded the Victoria Cross in recognition of his services in the Zulu War of 1879.

Gonville, born in 1845, was educated at Magnus Grammar School in Newark. Not surprisingly, he embarked on a career in the army and purchased a commission, joining the 2nd (Warwickshire) Battalion, 24th Regiment of Foot. In 1878, the battalion was sent to South Africa to aid colonists in their struggle against Xhosa tribesmen. When the senior officer of 'B' Company was wounded, Lieutenant Bromhead assumed command – just in time to participate in a new war.

In 1852, Britain had recognised the right of the Dutch Boers of the Transvaal to govern themselves as an independent state. The Boers were surrounded by various African tribes, with whom they seemed constantly to be at war. The most feared of these tribes was the Zulus, which lay to the south-east. From 1873, under a new warlike chief, Cetewayo, they posed a serious threat to the security of the Boers, who agreed to give up their independence for the promise of British protection – at least, until the Zulus were brought to heel.

On 11th January 1879, Lord Chelmsford led an army of over 16,000 men into the Zulu kingdom. He was joined by troops already in Africa, including the 2nd Warwickshires. Planning to encircle the enemy, he divided his force into three columns, thereby providing Cetewayo, who could call on up to 40,000 warriors, with an opportunity to tackle the British on a piecemeal basis.

The centre column crossed the border at a mission station called Rorke's Drift on the Buffalo River. Bromhead and 'B' Company were ordered to remain there on guard while the rest of the column advanced a further ten miles, to Isandlwana, where a camp was established. It was the sort of duty to which the men under Bromhead's command had become accustomed. He was not highly regarded by his superiors, who usually gave him undemanding tasks. This may have been the reason why his men disliked him. In the 1964 movie 'Zulu', he is played by Michael Caine, who portrays him as an aloof, detached individual. He *was* aloof, but this was owing to the fact that his hearing was failing. According to some sources, by the time of the campaign, he was almost completely deaf.

On 22 January, Chelmsford split his own centre column again, leaving around 1,800 men at Isandhwana, while he moved forward to reconnoitre. In the early afternoon, the ill-defended camp was attacked by 20,000 Zulus, who were under orders to kill anyone who wore a red coat. They obliged and the command was wiped out, the only European survivors being a few officers who happened to be wearing blue patrol jackets.

In mid-afternoon, news of the disaster reached Rorke's Drift. Bromhead was not the only officer present, for a Royal Engineer, Lieutenant John Chard had been delegated the task of looking after the cable river crossing. It may have come as a relief to Bromhead that Chard had seniority, although the two men appear to have worked well together.

At any rate, the decision was made to stand fast. To this end, defences were quickly established between two buildings, used as a store and field hospital respectively. An hour later, 4,000 Zulus hove into view and launched an immediate assault on the garrison, which numbered no more than 140 men.

Charge after charge was beaten back, although the British were forced to fall back to a secondary line of defence. Fighting continued through the hours of darkness, Bromhead, armed with a rifle, standing alongside his men. Finally, at about 4.00am the next morning, the Zulus withdrew. Their dead were numbered in the hundreds, for the cost of 17 British lives.

Later that morning, Chelmsford arrived with the remains of his command. His supplies and reserves of ammunition gone, his invasion was at an end. Had the Zulus maintained their offensive, disaster could easily have been transformed into catastrophe, but Chelmsford was permitted to make a perilous retreat.

Pending a decision on future strategy, Rorke's Drift was reinforced and fortified, gaining the unofficial title of 'Fort Bromhead'. Bromhead himself became more uncommunicative then ever. He is reported as spending every day sitting on a stone and puffing away on his pipe. His reticence to discuss the battle in any way even extended to a refusal to tender an official report.

The heroic defence of Rorke's Drift was used by the authorities to mask the fiasco of Isandlwana, and a total of 11 Victoria Crosses were awarded. However, the 'top brass' has never entertained much enthusiasm for conferring the highest of awards for bravery. Sir Garnet Wolsey, who had been sent out to turn defeat into victory, distributed the decorations, although he held the opinion that the men had simply been doing their duty.

In addition, Rorke's Drift probably saved Bromhead's career. In the absence of the fame it brought him, he would surely have been pensioned off on account of his disability. Instead, first as a Captain and later as a Major, he continued to serve overseas, notably in Burma, where he participated in the 3rd Anglo-Burmese War and in India. It was here that he would die, at Camp Gabhaura, Allahabad after contracting typhoid, on 9th February 1891.

Bromhead's grave at Allahabad, gradually fell into disrepair. In Thurlby's Church of St. German, however, a memorial plaque and a stained glass window were dedicated to him. In 2014, a small collection of his letters sold at auction for £1,200. In 2016 the family home, Thurlby Hall, was up for sale.

'The Cleverest Man in the British Army'

Sir William Robertson was a prime example of a self-made man. He began his army career as a Private and rose through the ranks to become a Field Marshal – a remarkable feat, given his humble origins.

Robertson was born in the Lincolnshire village of Welbourn on 29th January 1860. His beginnings were not quite so lowly as one is sometimes led to believe, for his father was the proprietor of a tailor's shop and later became Welbourn's postmaster. In terms of the local social hierarchy, therefore, the family occupied a position that many of their fellow villagers could only envy. That they were not so well-off as they might have been was owing to the fact that there were seven children.

From the very beginning, William displayed a burning ambition to get on in life. In the village school, he became a monitor, receiving sixpence per week to help other pupils with their reading. It must have rankled with him when, on leaving school, he had to take a job as boot boy – cleaning boots and fetching and carrying – in the service of the Reverend John William King at Ashby Hall. He achieved something of a step-up when he moved to Deene Park in Northamptonshire, as a footman. This proved to be the turning point in his career, for this was a military household, the home of the Crimean War hero, the Earl of Cardigan. William decided that the army might provide him with the opportunities he craved.

He enlisted on 13th November 1877, and by 1885 had risen to the rank of Sergeant-Major. This, in itself, was a notable achievement, and as far as someone of William's antecedents was concerned, the end of the line. Although commissions were now attainable by written examination, a private income and the family background to go with it were still very useful appendages. Nevertheless, in 1888, he succeeded in being promoted to 2nd Lieutenant and was posted to India. He saw some action, but it was his talent as an administrator that secured his future.

Walnut Tree Cottage, Welbourne, childhood home of Sir William Robertson

Back in England in 1896, he entered the Staff College at Camberley and subsequently became a captain in the Intelligence Department at the war office. He served in South Africa in the Second Boer War (1899-1902), where his desire to 'get on' in life is illustrated by his reaction to not being given a medal. He complained about it and kept on complaining until he was made up to brevet Lieutenant-Colonel. In 1910, he became Commandant of the Staff College, which was followed by a period spent at the War Office as Director of Military Training. It was during this time that he gained the reputation of being 'the cleverest man in the British army'.

On the outbreak of the First World War in 1914, he was appointed Quartermaster General of the British Expeditionary Force, a post ideally suited to his abilities as an organiser. Then, in 1915, he returned to London as Chief of the Imperial General Staff. This was a role to which he was less suited, for it involved working closely with cabinet ministers, and the blunt Lincolnshire boy was not endowed with the diplomatic skills needed to play politics.

Much has been written about the questionable wisdom of the allied military strategy on the Western Front. Robertson and General Douglas Haigh, Commander-in-Chief of the BEF, believed in wearing down the enemy by a series of advances, 'each step being prepared', wrote Robertson, 'by a predominant artillery fire and great expenditure in ammunition.' He might have added that the plan would also involve a considerable expenditure in human life. They cannot be blamed for inventing the concept, for it only amounted to what they had both been taught at Camberley: the enemy had to be comprehensively defeated in the primary theatre of war. Working on this assumption, Robertson had little sympathy for the injection of men and materials into sideshows such as the ill-fated Gallipoli campaign of 1915.

Promoted to General in 1916, Robertson survived as Chief of the Imperial General Staff until February 1918, when he resigned after a breakdown in his working relationship with the Prime Minister, David Lloyd-George. He was appointed Commander-in-Chief of Eastern Command, covering the east of England. Four months later, he took charge of the Home Forces in their entirety. Following the Armistice, he was given command of British Army of the Rhine. When he relinquished this post in March 1920, he was made a Field Marshal, becoming the only career soldier to start at the bottom of the ladder and climb to the very top.

Robertson received many accolades and finished his military career in the ceremonial role of Gold Stick-in-waiting to the Royal Horse Guards. During the 1920s, he developed a number of business interests and, fittingly, served as President of the British Legion. At long last a wealthy man, he died in 1933. Today, his name lives on in the Sir William Robertson Academy, a co-educational school situated in Welbourn.

Chapter Seventeen

ENGINEERING LINCOLNSHIRE

John 'Longitude' Harrison

Lincolnshire has been home to several famous clock and watchmakers. Among the earliest were Guy Dickinson of Lincoln and John Watts of Stamford, both of whom were working in the mid-seventeenth century. A relatively late starter was Joseph Hinds, who established a clock making business in Stamford in 1825. He prospered to the extent that the business is still flourishing as F. Hinds, the high street chain of jewellers.

Many folk depended upon local church clocks to give them the time and the maintenance of church clocks was an important part of a clockmaker's duties. In terms of accuracy, a minute or two either way was of little consequence to most people on terra firma, but for mariners, the lack of a reliable clock to help determine longitude could – and did – lead to disaster. Unfortunately, it took a tragedy to focus minds on the subject.

This occurred in 1707, during the War of the Spanish Succession. A British fleet of fifteen vessels, commanded by Sir Cloudesley Shovell, attacked the French port of Toulon. The expedition was unsuccessful and Shovell turned for home on 29th September 1707. Beset by bad weather, the fleet nevertheless made it back to the English Channel, which was reached on 22nd October. However, owing to the fact that it was impossible to ascertain their longitude, the ships were off course and ran aground on rocks off the Scilly Isles. Four sank with the loss of up to 2,000 lives.

As a result of the catastrophe – all the worse because it had happened in coastal waters – a Board of Longitude was set up to examine the issue of establishing longitude. As so often happened, the problem was thrown open to public competition, with a prize of £20,000 being offered to anyone who could produce a device for determining longitude within 30 nautical miles. One of the competitors was a Lincolnshire clockmaker called John Harrison.

Harrison, born in 1693, was raised in the Lincolnshire village of Barrow-upon-Humber. A carpenter by trade, he had been fascinated by clocks from early childhood. During the 1720s he constructed a number of clocks with mechanisms fashioned from wood. One of these, commissioned for the stable block on the Brocklesby Park estate, is still keeping excellent time.

In 1730, he took up the challenge of the Longitude Board and set himself the task of making a 'sea clock' which, during any point during a sea voyage, could accurately give the time at Greenwich. This could then be compared with the 'local time', facilitating the calculation of a vessel's longitude. He managed to secure financial backing from a private source to enable him to build it. It took him five years. The Board of Longitude was sufficiently impressed with the final product to give it a trial. In 1736, it was tested on a voyage to Lisbon and performed well enough for the Board to advance Harrison the sum of £500 to so that he could make refinements.

A further five years of work failed to achieve the results that Harrison and the Board were looking for and he received a further advance to continue his work. And continue he did, only to end up having to go back to the drawing board. This came about with his realisation that the required degree of accuracy could be best obtained by using a much smaller timepiece, along the lines of a pocket watch.

Accordingly, he began anew, designing and making a 'sea watch' in six years. By the time it was completed, he was 68. When the Board accepted it for trials, his son, William, was given the task of testing its efficiency on a voyage to Jamaica, undertaken in 1761. It proved an unqualified success, but the Board was still not satisfied. The results, it was suggested, could be put down to sheer luck. Therefore, a second transatlantic voyage was made. It, too, proved successful but, even then, the Board quibbled over awarding the promised prize money.

The real problem lay in the fact that the instrument had been so long in production, and the Board had an eye to the fact that, for practical purposes, it would have to be mass produced. With this in mind, the Board's members awarded him £10,000, with the balance to be paid when he gave up the rights to his invention. Naturally enough, Harrison wanted to protect his work. After a lifetime spent developing it, he had no wish to see the profits going to others. As a last resort, he approached King George III, with whose support, he petitioned Parliament, which awarded him £8,750.

As the Longitude Board had anticipated, production problems meant that the 'chronometers' were introduced quite slowly, although others were able to improve on Harrison's design and speed up the manufacturing process.

John Harrison died in 1776. His incredible efforts in perfecting an instrument which has saved countless lives at sea were finally recognised in 2006, with the unveiling of a memorial stone in Westminster Abbey. The Church of England Primary School in Barrow-Upon-Humber is named after him, as is a train – *The John Longitude Harrison*. In addition, 'The John Harrison Foundation' is dedicated to promoting his life and work.

Frank Whittle

Frank Whittle was born in Coventry in 1907. His father was an engineer, which helps to explain young Frank's interest in aeronautics. In 1923, he joined the RAF as an apprentice aircraft mechanic and was sent to RAF Cranwell. In his spare time, he enjoyed building model aircraft – which displayed such skill that he was recommended for officer training, at Cranwell's RAF College, graduating in 1928.

The thesis he wrote as part of his studies at Cranwell formed the basis of his future work on the development of the jet engine. As an alternative to the propeller engine, he proposed a motor with a conventional piston engine to provide compressed air to a combustion chamber with an exhaust used to provide thrust. At increased altitudes, he argued, the lower outside air pressure would increase efficiency. For the time being, however, he pursued his flying career, joining 111 Squadron at Hornchurch. He was a daredevil pilot – and a daredevil pilot he remained.

In 1936, with the sanction of the Air Ministry, Whittle formed Power Jets Ltd., which enabled him to set to work developing his engine. Following successful trials in 1937-38, the Air Ministry finally placed an order for what was called the 'WU' engine. Gloster, contracted to make an aircraft for it, came up with the

The RAF College, Cranwell

E.28/39. It was designed as a fighter, with a wingspan of 29 feet (8.84m) and a steerable nosewheel. Rover, working to Whittle's specifications, was supposed to produce the engine, but delays led to Whittle putting one together himself from an array of spare parts. On 8th April 1941, the finished product, piloted by Gloster's Chief Test Pilot, Gerry Sayer, made a series of short hops on the company's test site at Brockworth. Another trial was made on 15th May, on this occasion from RAF Cranwell, where the E.28/39 flew for 17 minutes, reaching a speed of 340mph.

This is often claimed to be the first flight of an aircraft powered by a jet engine. In fact, the first such flight was made on 27th August 1939, by a German pilot, Erich Warsitz, in a Heinkel He178. In Germany, the jet-engine designer, Hans von Ohain, had been working along parallel lines to Whittle and, while Whittle had been working within the constraints of his own cash-strapped company, von Ohain had been fortunate in gaining the backing of Heinkel.

However, Whittle and von Ohain did experience similar problems when it came to drumming up government interest. Further difficulties arose when other engine companies in both countries set up rival programmes – and the development of the jet-powered fighter plane grew into a no-holds-barred race. In Britain, for example, while Rover worked on Whittle's engine, the company secretly set up its own programme to produce an 'improved' version.

Owing to the problems he was experiencing with Rover, Whittle turned to Rolls Royce. The company was able to help in solving a few persistent technical problems and assumed responsibility for the production of his engine. Work was speeded up, but the Germans stayed ahead and the Luftwaffe threatened to regain the initiative in the air with the introduction of the jet-powered Messerschmitt Me262, which first flew operationally in April 1944.

By the time jet-powered fighters took to the air, Whittle and von Ohain had each lost control of his brain child. During trials in April 1943, Whittle himself floated the idea that jet engine development should be nationalised. The Air Ministry opted for the nationalisation of Power Jets only. It was a shrewd move, for Power Jets was, after all, the driving force behind the technology. After some haggling, the Ministry took possession of the company for just over £135,000. Whittle, who received £10,000 for his own shares, was retained as Chief Technical Adviser. His health had never been robust and he spent several months during 1944 recovering from nervous exhaustion.

The successor to the Gloucester E.28/39, the Gloucester Meteor, became operational in July 1944, with 616 Squadron at RAF Manston. The Messerschmitt Me262, although very effective in combat, was far less durable than its British rival which had Rolls Royce manufactured engines that could run for 150 hours without a major overhaul, as opposed to the 25 hour lifespan of the Me 262 Junkers engines. However, although the Meteors proved useful in knocking out Flying Bombs, the remaining months of the war were essentially a time for ironing out problems.

After the war, Whittle resigned from Power Jets. He retired from the RAF (having attained the rank of Air Commodore) in 1948, in which year he also received a knighthood. Even then, his work was appreciated more widely in America than in Britain, and he subsequently worked and lived there. When he died, in 1976, his ashes were returned home for interment in the Memorial Chapel of RAF Cranwell's Church of St. Michael & All Angels.

Raymond Mays

There is no doubt that Raymond Mays 'belongs' to Lincolnshire, for he was born in Eastgate House in Bourne in 1899 and was still residing there when he died in 1980. His is not quite a household name, but it should be because he put British motor racing on the map.

The son of a successful industrialist, Mays was educated at Oundle School and then, following a period of service in the army, Christ's College, Cambridge where he read engineering – and where he also began his motor racing career.

Motor racing in the 1920s was a well established sport, the Brooklands circuit having opened in 1907. Throughout the 1920s, the 'Bentley Boys', an assortment of well-heeled enthusiasts who drove Bentley sports cars, put Britain in the international frame with several victories in the Le Mans 24-hour event. Then, as now, the sport was very much a preserve of the wealthy.

One branch of motor sport which allowed for a little more flexibility in terms of participation was hill climbing, in which a wide variety of cars would compete against the clock to make the fastest time over a given distance on a winding, uphill stretch. The most famous of these courses was (and still is) Shelsley Walsh in Worcestershire. Raymond Mays competed at both Brooklands, where he won a handicap event in 1921, and at Shelsley Walsh where, in 1923, he posted a course record – the first of many successes.

Motor racing ace, Raymond Mays, pictured (far left) with his English Racing Automobiles team at Bourne in 1935. (Bourne Civic Society)

In 1933, Mays and two partners set up 'English Racing Automobiles' (ERA), with the aim of designing and racing a car of their own. The Germans had monopolised the inter-war years' equivalent of Formula One with massive Auto Union and Mercedes Benz cars, which bore a passing resemblance to First World War tanks on wheels. ERA could not hope to complete and wisely concentrated on the smaller 1.5 litre class, which was generally better suited to hill climbing courses. The company enjoyed many successes both at home and on the continent – Mays himself winning the Eifelrennen at Germany's Nürburgring Stadium in 1935.

In 1939, despite ERA's considerable success, Mays withdrew from the team and formed another company, Automobile Development Ltd., with a view to manufacturing a new Grand Prix car. His plans were interrupted by the Second World War, but resurrected in 1945. With money in short supply, it proved a challenging task, Mays using all his powers of persuasion to acquire the necessary sponsorship. Meanwhile, Mays continued driving, winning the first British Hill Climb Championship in 1947. He also found time to establish 'Raymond Mays & Partners Ltd' in Bourne, a car dealership specialising in Rolls Royce and Bentleys.

In 1949, Automobile Development Ltd., was renamed 'British Racing Motors Ltd' (BRM), and Mays demonstrated its first car, the 'Type 15', using the nearby Folkingham airfield as a track. The 1.5 litre 'V16' engine was not a success and although the car did win at Goodwood in 1950, the problems mounted until BRM was forced to sell out to the Rubery Owen engineering company.

Mays retired from driving in 1950. From 1952, when Rubery Owen acquired BRM, although Mays was still very actively involved, he was able to spend time expanding his car showroom business, to which he added a Ford dealership which led to him adapting Ford models for saloon car racing. However, BRM's difficulties continued throughout the 1950s, until Rubery Owen, in their turn, were considering whether to throw in the towel.

Finally, in 1961, a decision was taken to streamline the management of the company – at the expense of Mays and his long-time partner, Peter Berthon. It appeared to pay off for, in 1962, BRM won the Constructors' World Championship, with Graham Hill taking the drivers' title. Raymond Mays' dream had finally reached fruition.

BRM continued into the 1970s, and in 1971 took second place in the constructor rankings. However, it never again achieved the success of the 1962 season. The company folded in 1977, by which time McLaren and Williams were ready to fly the flag for Britain in a sport which they would dominate throughout the 1980s and 1990s.

In 1978, Raymond Mays received a richly deserved CBE for services to motor sport. He died two years later, a lonely and increasingly isolated figure. A plaque adorns the exterior wall of the imposing Eastbourne House. A floor of Bourne's Baldock Mill Heritage Centre is dedicated to Mays' life and work, while a memorial nearby commemorates both Mays and Bourne's motor racing heritage. A southern relief road for the town is named 'Raymond Mays Way'. The old ERA works were long-ago incorporated into Delaine's bus garage site. Mays' garage survived until 2005 when its owners could sadly no longer compete with local supermarket petrol prices.

Chapter Eighteen

MYSTERIOUS LINCOLNSHIRE

The Witches of Belvoir

Sir Francis Manners succeeded to the title of Earl of Rutland in 1612, taking possession of Belvoir Castle in Leicestershire. An enlightened nobleman, he took his responsibilities seriously, and the castle became, it was said, 'a daily reception for all sorts both rich and poor, especially such auncient people as neighboured the same'. Among those to benefit from the Earl's munificence were Joan Flower and her two daughters, Margaret and Phillipa, who were given employment in the household. Joan and Phillipa were used as general 'chair-women', and continued to reside in the local village of Bottesford; Margaret looked after the poultry and the 'wash-house' and lived-in at the castle.

In terms of the duties they performed, the women were not high up the pecking order, but the relative favour shown to them must have created some resentment among their fellow villagers, who were quick to spread hostile gossip. Joan Flower, they asserted, was 'a monstrous malicious woman, full of oathes, curses and imprecations irreligious'. She terrified her neighbours 'with curses and threatening revenge', giving rise to suspicions that she was 'a notorious witch'. Phillipa, meanwhile, 'lewdly transported' with a man called Thomas Simpson who claimed that his lover had 'bewitched' him, while Margaret, they averred, often stole from the castle. Eventually, Katherine, Countess of Rutland bowed to the pressure and stopped Margaret from 'lying any more in the Castle'. However, she did give Margaret forty shillings, a bolster and 'a mattresse of wooll', which suggests that she did not feel too badly disposed towards the girl.

A little time after this occurrence, the Earl and his immediate family became subject to 'sicknesse and extraordinary convulsions'. The eldest son, Henry, Lord Ross, 'sickened very strangely' and died; his younger brother, Francis, was also 'severely tormented'. The logical conclusion was that these circumstances had been brought about by Joan, Margaret and Phillipa Flower, through a series of 'incantations, spells and charms', in revenge for what they considered to be their ill-treatment. As a result, they were arrested around Christmas 1617 and examined by Justices of the Peace, who sent them for trial at Lincoln's Lent Assizes.

Joan Flower did not reach Lincoln. According to a contemporary pamphlet entitled 'The Wonderful Discoverie of the Witchcrafts of Margaret and Phillip (sic) Flower', she died en route in the Roman settlement of Ancaster. She had asked for some bread and butter and, after wishing that 'it would never go through her' if she were guilty, she collapsed and died 'with a horrible excruciation of soule and body'. The simple explanation would be that, half-starved, she ate too quickly and choked to death, but the establishment imposed a more elaborate interpretation on the incident: witches, it was argued were unable to eat bread, owing to its sacramental qualities. Joan's death in attempting to digest it was, in itself, proof of her guilt.

Margaret and Phillipa were left to face the music alone. Duly encouraged, in all probability, by the cruelty of their accusers, they confessed to the role they had played in bringing about the death of Henry. Joan had asked Margaret to bring her one of the child's gloves, with which she stroked her cat, 'Rutterkin'. Later, she dipped the glove in hot water, and 'prickt it often'. A similar procedure was followed for Francis. A third spell was cast on the Countess so that she might bear no more children. For this, Joan used a pair of gloves and some wool from the mattress given to Margaret. After soaking these ingredients in a mixture of warm water and blood, she again rubbed them on the cat. It was presumed that 'Rutterkin' was Joan's 'familiar' evil spirit (having the same function as 'Graymalkin', owned by the First Witch in *Macbeth*).

Tried before Sir Henry Hobart and Sir Edward Bromley, the sisters were found guilty of 'confessing themselves actors in the destruction of Henry, Lord Rosse' and were hanged on 11th March 1618.

Young Francis died in 1620, and the Countess of Rutland bore no more children. The Earl of Rutland died in 1632. His family monument in the church of St Mary the Virgin in Bottesford bears an inscription stating that his wife bore him two sons, 'both of which dyed in their infancy by wicked practice and sorcerye'. Did he really believe this?

The story makes a little more sense when it is placed in context. King James's interest in witchcraft was well known. In 1597, he had published a work entitled 'Daemonologie', which became the standard text for witch-hunters in Britain. The Earl of Rutland occupied a prominent position at Court – in April 1616, he was made a Knight of the Garter and, a year later, became a Privy Councillor. It would be unwise for an ambitious courtier to pour scorn on the notion of witchcraft and it is probable that, in presenting himself as a victim of sorcery, Rutland saw a way of turning the tragedy of his son's death to advantage.

'Old Jeffrey'

In 1697, owing to the influence of Queen Mary, Samuel Wesley, Church of England clergyman, poet and father of John Wesley (see page 98) was appointed to the living of Epworth. When he arrived at the Rectory, he and his wife already had four children. In the coming years, another fifteen would be born, of which ten would survive to adulthood.

The family had been living at the Rectory for almost twenty years when there occurred a series of inexplicable paranormal events. In residence at the time (in addition to the family servants) were Samuel and his wife (Susanna) and seven of their children: Emilia, Susanna, Mary, Mehetabel ('Hetty'), Anne, Martha, and Kazziah ('Kezzie').

The ghostly phenomena began on the evening of 1st December 1716. Anne and Susanna Wesley were sitting in the dining room when they heard a strange rushing sound (later likened to the turning of a windmill) coming from the direction of the garden. This was followed by a series of loud knocks, in distinct groups of three, on the ceiling – repeated nightly for two weeks. They were heard by everyone except Samuel Wesley, and when his daughters informed him of their experiences, he treated it all as a joke. From 21st December, however, Samuel himself began to hear the rhythmic rappings, but his efforts to track them to their source always failed.

In addition to the sounds, things were seen – a white rabbit, a creature resembling a badger and the figure of a man in a loose, trailing nightgown which was encountered on the stairs and in various rooms. Emilia thought of calling it 'Jeffrey' and the name stuck. It was assumed that 'Jeffrey' was a spirit, responsible for creating the phenomena experienced by all the members of the household, including the servants. From time to time, they attempted to communicate with it. When the rappings were heard, for example, Mrs Wesley would knock in response. On other occasions, her husband tried to engage it in conversation, but to no avail. Neither were visitors to the house spared a demonstration. Samuel prevailed upon Joseph Hoole, vicar of nearby Haxey, to spend a night in the Rectory. The two men spent the evening following the knocking noises – as always, presented in groups of three – from room to room.

'Jeffrey' seemed especially averse to Wesley's conduct of morning family prayers, which always included a prayer for King George I. On these occasions, the rappings would rise in a crescendo. So incensed was 'Jeffrey' upon hearing the name of the monarch that he would resort to physical violence, pushing Wesley around the house and jostling his plate while he was dining. These were the days of the Jacobite Rebellions, aimed at the restoration of the Stuart dynasty, which implied that the spirit had pronounced Jacobite sympathies.

Friends and colleagues, some of whom experienced the phenomena for themselves, advised Wesley to pack his bags and leave, but he stuck it out, proclaiming that he would never flee from the devil. Eventually, the disturbances did die down until finally, by the middle of January 1717 – just over twelve months after they had begun – they had almost ceased.

So, how can the strange happenings in Epworth Rectory be explained? Most of the family believed a spirit to be responsible. Mrs Wesley thought it might be the spirit of one of her three sons, very much alive and away at school at the time. The girls, on the other hand, suggested a deceased evil spirit, intent on punishing the household for their father's preaching. Another set of theories involve the suggestion of trickery, for which either the servants, hostile neighbours or the Wesley girls themselves were responsible. The Reverend W B Stonehouse, author of *The History of the Isle of Axholme*, thought that all the noises were created by 'some piece of machinery' in the attic 'which required to be wound up before the performance began.' Here, it may be worth noting that Wesley's Anglican High Church practices and Tory politics did not endear

Epworth Rectory, home of the Reverend Charles Wesley and his family

him to his rustic parishioners. In 1709, he and his family had barely escaped from the Rectory when it was almost entirely destroyed by a fire of suspicious origin.

An interesting physical theory for the phenomena involves the effects of underground water. Gypsum had once been mined in the area, and it has been suggested that some of the filling from the long disused quarries had been washed out, allowing the tidal influence of the River Trent (which extends as far as Epworth) to cause rumblings and movement. Currently, the most favoured explanation identifies 'Old Jeffrey' as a poltergeist. The poltergeist (or 'noisy ghost') is a mischievous spirit, confined to a particular house or locality, and which is able to utilise the latent energy of adolescent children. Alternatively, it is identified as a secondary personality of such an individual. In this case, Hetty is identified as the focus of the activity. Although much of the phenomena does seem to have revolved around her, she was 19 years of age when it all started and, correspondingly, perhaps a little long in the tooth.

Whatever the explanation may be, the haunting of Epworth Rectory is Lincolnshire's most celebrated true ghost story, and there must scarcely be a visitor to the home of the Wesleys who does not secretly harbour a wish to catch just a fleeting glimpse of 'Old Jeffrey' himself.

Airfield Ghosts

The appearance of ghosts can often be traced back to emotive and violent events. It would appear to follow, therefore, that venues such as battlefields and wartime airfields should be among the most haunted in the country.

Even so, airfield ghosts are not limited to airfields. Aircrew, for example, had their favourite inns and public houses. With village pubs now going out of business at the rate of about 30 per week, it is inevitable that some of these watering holes have now vanished. *The Cross Keys* in South Killingholme, frequented by crew from 550 Squadron based at RAF North Killingholme, has been demolished, while Binbrook's *Marquis of Granby*, once a port of call for 460 Squadron, has been converted into a house. *The Monks Arms* (closed in 2000), an iconic landmark at Caenby Corner, was said to be haunted by the ghost of an airman from nearby RAF Hemswell. In Welton, *The Black Bull* (which has survived) is also haunted by an airman. Initially, the ghost, clad in a leather flying jacket, was said to be associated with nearby RAF Dunholme Lodge, but later versions of the story suggest RAF Scampton.

The best-known haunting in this setting is undoubtedly that associated with 'The Petwood', Woodhall Spa. The imposing building was originally a private residence, designed for Baroness Grace von Eckhardstein. During the First World War, it was used as a convalescent home for wounded servicemen.

In the Second World War, it was requisitioned as an RAF Officers' Mess – most famously for 617 Squadron of RAF Woodhall Spa. The hotel contains much   memorabilia including (outside) a 'bouncing bomb' casing. Officers of 617 Squadron, including Guy Gibson, are alleged to haunt the hotel's 'Lancaster Bar', with the sound of laughter and clinking glasses echoing along the corridors long after it has closed for the night.

Among the most haunted airfield structures are the few surviving watch towers. Lights are sometimes seen emanating from the cavernous remains of the watch tower of RAF Coleby Grange, and the ghostly figure of an airman has often been seen in the vicinity. The ghost of an American flyer haunts the watch tower at RAF East Kirkby and an eerie presence, sometimes heralded by a blast of cold air, haunts RAF Bardney's watch tower. The watch tower situated at RAF Elsham Wolds has long since been demolished, but in the years following the Second World War it was used as a domestic dwelling, and the family living there became accustomed to seeing the apparition of an airman wandering in and out of the rooms.

Much ghostly phenomena has been experienced at RAF Hemswell. Its pre-war architecture is still intact and, although many buildings have been put to retail use, it can be a ghostly place after hours. Two airmen are regularly encountered at the old main gate. It has been suggested that they are en route to the Officers' Mess, which still stands at the other side of the A631. Much of RAF Binbook's infrastructure also survives. Unlike Hemswell, however, a good many of the old buildings lie empty. It is an eerie spot even in daylight. The resident ghost has been christened 'Clubfoot'. Apparently, he was an Australian member of

The shell of the Watch Tower, allegedly haunted by the ghosts of wartime aircrew, is all that remains of RAF Coleby Grange

the ground staff who was injured by the manoeuvres of a careless pilot. By way of revenge, he tried to attach an explosive device to the pilot's aircraft, but succeeded only in blowing himself up. He is occasionally seen limping along the perimeter track.

The late comedian, Michael Bentine, used to tell the story of a ghost he met during his wartime days at RAF Wickenby. Returning from leave late one night, he was walking towards his Nissen hut when he passed a flight lieutenant who he knew well. Acknowledging him, Bentine entered the hut and went to bed. The next morning, he learned that the man he had encountered only a few hours before had, in fact, died when his Lancaster crashed two days earlier.

Of course, ghosts can be detected through senses other than that of sight. The sound of music, accompanied by laughter has been heard drifting across the tarmac at RAF Hemswell, while the sound of Rolls Royce Merlin engines have been heard on many a deserted Lincolnshire airfield. Similarly, the ghost of a pipe-smoking airman has been reported in Austacre Wood, site of the bomb dump at RAF Bardney. Nothing is ever seen, but visitors have picked up the unmistakable aroma of pipe tobacco coming from the trees. Sometimes, presences can simply be felt and, the solitary rambler, traversing an expanse of crumbling runway in the fading light of a winter's afternoon, rarely completes his journey without casting an uneasy glance or two over his shoulder.

Ghost Trains

Talk of railway ghosts inevitably conjures up images of Arnold Ridley's stage play *The Ghost Train* and Charles Dickens' classic short story *The Signalman*. While both are works of fiction, an examination of the history of Lincolnshire's railways suggest that stranger things have actually happened...

The East Lincolnshire Railway, linking Grimsby with Boston, was opened in 1848. In 1905, six halts were added to the northern portion of the line, between Grimsby and Louth. One of these was located at Utterby, along Pear Tree Lane. The old Utterby crossing was supposedly haunted by the ghost of one John Edward Lancaster.

Lancaster worked on the railway. On a foggy day in January 1953, he was walking southbound along the track. He had reached the level crossing at Utterby when he was struck and killed instantly by a passing train. Several accounts place him in the path of a freight train, while others suggest that in trying to avoid the freight train (which he must have heard approaching) he stepped in front of a passenger train. From time to time, what is believed to be Lancaster's ghost was seen in the vicinity of the halt. Occasionally, the tale is embellished by experiences of motorists whose vehicles unaccountably broke down on the crossing. The A16 now runs along the route of the old track.

A ghost train used to haunt the Manchester, Sheffield and Lincolnshire Railway line connecting Grimsby with Doncaster. Accounts refer to an accident which occurred at some time during the 1920s. A passenger train derailed near the Ancholme Bridge section (opened in 1866), killing a number of people. Visibility was poor at the time, and on several occasions since then, whenever fog has descended on this portion of the track, a glowing, spectral engine has been sighted.

In one version of the story, the accident happened because the driver and fireman were fighting. This detail may have its origins with an accident which happened in Grantham in 1906, when an express passenger train ran off the rails, coming to rest in Old Wharf Road. A surviving passenger claimed to have been told that, when the incident occurred, the driver and fireman could be seen having an argument on the footplate.

Another ghost train is said to run on the Louth to Bardney Railway. The line was a late starter, not fully opening until 1876. It

Site of the railway station at Hallington, said to be occasionally frequented by a ghost train

ceased catering for passengers in 1951, and closed down altogether in 1960. The phantom train – said to be a goods train – is wholly an audio phenomenon. It is never seen, but residents of Hallington, the site of the first station from Louth have reported hearing it drawing to a halt and letting off steam at the station which was situated on the minor road between Hallington and Raithby. It is also heard labouring uphill towards the tunnel at Withcall.

There are many ghostly tales associated with Lincolnshire's signal boxes, where signalmen often worked long shifts in rural isolation. Footsteps were regularly heard to ascend the stairs leading up to the box at Kirton-in-Lindsey, on the Manchester, Sheffield & Lincolnshire line, but whenever the occupant looked out, there was never anyone there.

The signal box at Claxby, on the Market Rasen branch line of the Great Grimsby & Sheffield Junction Railway, is occasionally haunted by the ghost of a signalman who passed away in the box during an evening shift. The sounds of stentorian breathing, and even sightings of the deceased man have been reported.

A ghost story concerning a signal box, which can be traced back to its source, concerns Barkston Junction on the East Coast line near Grantham. In August 1961, the sound recordist, Peter Handford (who won an Academy Award for his work on *Out of Africa*), arranged to record some train sounds in the vicinity of the Barkston South box, which would be unmanned during the night. However, when he arrived on site, he noticed that the signal box door was ajar, so he went inside. An individual who he took to be a signalman, sat looking out of the window and expressed little interest in why Handford was there. Instead, he began to talk about an unsolved murder which had been committed locally. Handford left and spent the night making his recordings. When he had finished, he returned to the signal box to find it locked and empty. Staff at Grantham Station later confirmed that no one had been on duty in the box on the night in question. (There were once 10,000 signal boxes nationwide, a number that has been reduced to 500, with more cuts on the way. Of the survivors, many are classed as listed buildings, 18 of which are in Lincolnshire.)

Today, the vast majority of Lincolnshire's level crossing gates are operated automatically but, prior to the 1960s, when automation was introduced, gates used to be opened and closed manually – work that required the services of crossing keepers, who would often operate from wooden huts. On one occasion during the 1920s, a railway porter was sent to cover the shift of the crossing keeper at Hibaldstow, (Manchester, Sheffield & Lincolnshire line) who had called in sick. The man was struggling to open one of the crossing gates when he was run down and killed by a train. From then on, footsteps would often be heard in the vicinity of the cabin, with no explanation ever being discovered for the phenomenon. Ironically, in 2007, Network Rail staged and filmed a crash at Hibaldstow crossing as part of their campaign to discourage motorists from jumping red lights at automated barriers.

BIBLIOGRAPHY

Anon, *The Life and Death of Gamaliel Ratsey*, 1605 (OUP, 1935).

Anon, *Some Recollections of Jean Ingelow and Her Early Friends* (Wells Gardner, Darton & Co., 1901)

Barnes, I, *The Wonderful Discoverie of the Witchcrafts of Maragret & Phillip Flower* (1619)

Batchelor, John, *Tennyson: To strive, to seek, to find* (Chatto & Windus, 2012)

Brammer, Betty, *Winceby and the Battle* (Richard Kay, 1994)

Bryant, Peter, *Grimsby Chums* (Humberside Leisure Services, 1991)

Butlin, Sir Billy, *The Billy Butlin Story* (Robson Books, 1982)

Butter, Nathaniell, *The Life, Confession and Heartie Repentance of Francis Cartwright, Gentleman* (W. Stansby, 1621)

Campbell, John, *The Iron Lady: Margaret Thatcher* (Vintage, 2012)

Clark, David, *The Bretwalda Guide to Second World War Airfields in Lincolnshire* (Bretwalda Books Ltd., 2015)

Cox, J. Charles, *Lincolnshire* (Methuen & Co Ltd., 1916)

Cullen, Tom, *The Prostitute's Padre* (The Bodley Head Co., Ltd., 1975)

Foxe, John, *The Acts and Monuments Online* (www.johnfoxe.org)

Golley, John, *Whittle: The True Story* (Airlife Publishing, 1987)

Griggs, Frederick, *Highways and Byways in Lincolnshire* (MacMillan & Co., Ltd., 1914)

Hall, Rev. George, *The Gypsy's Parson* (Sampson, Low, Marston & Co., Ltd., 1915)

Hancock, T. N., *Bomber County* (Lincolnshire Library Service, 1978)

Holmes, Clive, *Seventeenth Century Lincolnshire* (Society for Lincolnshire History & Archaeology, 1980)

Halpenny, Bruce Barrymore, *Ghost Stations: Lincolnshire* (L'Aquila, 2012)

Marratt, William, *The History of Lincolnshire* (William Marratt, 1814)

Martin, Sean, *The Knights Templar* (Pocket Essentials, 2009)

Matthews, Derek, *William Marwood, The Gentleman Executioner* (Eastprint Publishing, 2010)

Mays, Raymond, *Split Second: My Racing Years* (Foulis, 1951)

Mee, Arthur, *The King's England: Lincolnshire* (Hodder & Stoughton Ltd., 1949)

212

Morgan, Ian, *Tom Otter and the Slaying of Mary Kirkham* (Ian Morgan, 2012)

Morris, Donald R., *The Washing of the Spears* (Jonathan Cape, 1966)

Morton, H.V., *In Search of England* (Methuen & Co. Ltd., 1927)

O'Brien, Patrick, *Joseph Banks* (Harvill Press, 1997)

Price, David A., *Love & Hate in Jamestown* (Vintage, 2005)

Rex, Peter, *Hereward* (Amberley Publishing, 2005)

Robertson, Field Marshal Sir William, *From Private to Field Marshal* (Constable, 1921)

Sobel, Dara, *Longitude* (Harper Perennial, 2005)

Southworth, Pamela, *Delaney The Cat Burglar* (Richard Kay, 2005)

Stennett, Alan, *Lost Railways of Lincolnshire* (Countryside Books, 2007)

Storey, Neil R., *Zeppelin Blitz* (The History Press, 2015)

Thompson, Pishey, *The History and Antiquities of Boston* (Longman & Co., 1856)

Treherne, John, *Dangerous Precincts* (Jonathan Cape, 1987)

Tomkins, Stephen, *John Wesley* (Lion Publishing PLC, 2003)

Trollope, Edward, *Sleaford and the Wapenlakes of Flaxwell and Aswardhurn* (W. Kent, 1872)

Trundle, John, *Three Bloodie Murders 1613* (EEBO Edition, 2010)

West, John, *Oliver Cromwell and The Battle of Gainsborough* (Richard Kay, 1992)

White, Michael, *Isaac Newton, The Last Sorcerer* (Fourth Estate Ltd., 1997)

White, William, *White's 1856 Lincolnshire* (David & Charles, 1969)

Young, Peter, *Edgehill 1642* (Roundwood Press Ltd., 1967)

INDEX

Airfields   88–91, 122–8, 135–8
Airfield ghosts   206–8
Alfred, Lord Tennyson 148–152
American missile bases   136
Ancholme Bridge   209
Anwick   22
Appleby Magna   105
Armoured vehicles   82–5
Askew, Anne   95–7
Avro Lancaster   126
Axholme, Isle of   2

Banks, Sir Joseph   142–5
Barkston Junction   211
Barrow-upon-Humber 192, 193
Battles
    Gainsborough   40–43
    Lincoln   35–8
    Losecoat Field   38–40
    Winceby Fight   43–6
Belvoir, witches of   200–202
Bolingbroke Castle   43–6
Bomber Command   124–6,
    129–133
Boston   152, 153, 156, 157
Bottesford   200, 202
Bourne   158, 172, 179, 196–9

Brides of Enderby   153
Bromhead,
    Lt-Gen., Sir Gonville   185–7
Buffalo Bill   65–7
Bull Run, Stamford   56–8
Burghley House   173
Butlin, Billy   67–70
Byard's Leap   14–17

Caistor Gad Whip   63
Cartwright, Francis   47–50
Churches   6–8
Cleethorpes Pier   72
Cleethorpes cemetery   87
Coningsby village   9

Dashwood, Sir Francis   30–31
Davidson, Harold   71–2
Delaney, Robert Augustus
    'Gussie'   165–7
Digby   123, 125, 128
Dodd, Rev. William   158–161
Drake Stones   21
Dunston Pillar   29–31

Eisenhower, General   127
Epworth   98, 203, 205
Executioner,
    William Marwood   53–5

Fabian of the Yard 165
Farming 5-6
Fens 2, 23-6
Fishing 6
Fonaby Sack Stone 21
Foxe's Book of Martyrs 154-7
Franklin, Sir John 111-115, 149

Gadsby, Frank 'Peggy' 74-5
Gainsborough, Battle of 40-43
Gargoyles 18
Gibson, Guy 128-9
Gilbert of Sempringham 92-4
Gilbertine Order 93-4
Grantham 141, 176, 177
Grimsby 85, 86, 87
Grimsby Chums 79-82
Gypsy's Parson 101-4

HMS Royal Arthur 69
Hall, George 101-4
Hallington 210
Harris, Sir Arthur 'Bomber' 130-131
Harrison, John 191-3
Haxey Hood 58-61
Hemswell 123
Hereward the Wake 179-181
Hibaldstow 211
Highwaymen 161-4

Hinchliffe, Captain Walter Raymond 115-121
Hinds, Joseph 191
Holbeach 146
Horncastle 101, 145, 170
Illingworth, Rev. Cayley 145
Imp 17-18
Ingelow, Jean 152-4

John, King, lost treasure 13-14
Julian's Bower 32-4

Kendall, Reverend Thomas 169
King Stephen incident 86
Kirkstead 106
Kirton-in-Lindsey 123
Knights Templar 26-9

Lancaster, John Edward 209
'Little Willie' 82-5
Lindsey, Earl of 182-4
Lincoln
  Aircraft production 88
  Battle of 35-8
  Brayford Wharf 5
  Imp 17-18
  Sir Joseph Banks Conservatory 145
  Tank manufacture 82-5
  Statue of Tennyson 149
  Usher Gallery 18

Lincolnshire Rising 168-172
Losecoat Field, Battle of 38-40
Louth 169
Lovell, Thomas 23
Lucan, Arthur 76-8

Mablethorpe 150
MacKay, Elsie 116-120
Manby 123
Marsh 2
Marwood, William 53-5
Mays, Raymond 135, 196-9
Moore, Charles 105

Newton, Sir Isaac 139-141
North-west Passage 111-115

'Old Jeffrey' 203-6
Old Mother Riley 76-8
Operation Chastise 132-3
Operation Overlord 127
Operation Market Garden 128

Pals brigades 79-82
Pelham's Pillar 29
Pier divers 73-5
Piers 72-5
Pocahontas 108-111

RAF Cranwell 122, 194
Revesby Abbey 142, 144, 145
RNAS Killingholme 88-91

Robert Bertie, Earl of Lindsey 182-4
Robertson, Sir William 188-190
Royal Flying Corps 88-91
Royal Naval Air Service 88-90
Ruckland 101
Ratsey, Gamaliel 161-4
Rye, Fred 67, 71-2
Sandtoft 134
Scampton 123, 128, 132, 146
Sempringham 92-4
Skegness 70-72
Smith, John 108-111
Somersby 148-150
Sopwith Camel 89-91
Spilsby 111, 114, 124
Stallingborough 95
Stamford 191
Stamford Bull Run 56-8
Strugglers Inn 55
Storr, Rev. William 47-8
Stukeley, William 145-7
Swineshead 165
Tattershall Castle 10
Temple Bruer 26-9
Tennyson, statue of 149
Thatcher, Margaret 176-8
Thurlby Hall 185, 187
Tom Otter's Gibbet 50-52

Turf Maze	32-4	William Cecil, Lord Burghley	172-5
Usher, James Ward	18	William Foster & Co	82-5
Usher Gallery	18, 19	Winceby Fight	43-6
Utterby	209	Winceby Stone	20
Victoria Cross	129, 131, 133	Wolds	1-2
Waddington	123	Woodhall Spa	130-1
Wakeford, John	104-7	Woolsthorpe-by-Colsterworth	139-141
Washing Molly Grime	61		
Welbourn	188, 189, 190	Vermuyden, Cornelius	24-5
Wesley, John	98-101, 203		
Whittle, Frank	194-6	Yellowbelly	9-11
		Zeppelin raids	85-8

About the author

David Clark had a career as an English and history teacher. A battlefield historian, he has written several books on the subject of British battlefields including *A Brief Guide to British Battlefields* (Robinson 2015), covering over a hundred British battlefield sites.

He has lived with his wife Alice in Lincolnshire since his retirement and he was born and brought up just across the River Humber, in Hull. His mother's family were Lincolnshire people, and his grandfather built the extension to Trinity Methodist Church in Barton-upon-Humber in 1905.

His first Lincolnshire book was *Second World War Airfields in Lincolnshire* (Bretwalda Books 2015). David is a keen gardener and exhibits at agricultural shows.

Also published by Merlin Unwin Books

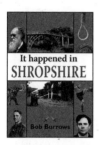

It Happened in Shropshire
Bob Burrows

It Happened in Shropshire is a vibrant and compelling account of the county's diverse heritage; its heroes, its battles, its discoveries, its crimes.

'An invaluable, readable and informative guide to the county.'
– Shropshire Life   £8.99

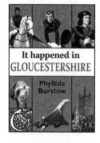

It Happened in Gloucestershire
Phyllida Barstow

Barstow's lively prose transports the reader across the county: from its stunning cathedral to its swan lake at Slimbridge, taking us surfing the Severn Bore, tumbling down Cooper's Hill on the notorious Cheese Race, round the challenging course at Badminton and to Imjin Hill, site of the tragic stand of the Glorious Glosters.   £7.99

It Happened in Lancashire
Malcolm Greenhalgh

From the world's largest tripe factory to the Battle of Wigan Lane; from the Peterloo massacre to the first British canal – Lancashire can claim it all.
It was one of the poorest parts of Britain due to its difficult terrain, poor soil, estuaries and bogs, but it went on to become one of the wealthiest through coal, cotton and slavery.
It has suffered some of the greatest tragedies: the massacre of the Accrington Pals in 30 minutes of the First World War; countless pit disasters; the pounding of the Blitz.
But it replied by producing some of the greatest comedians: from George Formby to Ken Dodd to Peter Kay. Not to mention the many great cricketers, rugby players and footballers.
                                            £7.99

For details of our full range of countryside books see:
www.merlinunwin.co.uk